BUYING FOR ARMAGEDDON

THE ARNOLD AND CAROLINE ROSE MONOGRAPH SERIES
OF THE AMERICAN SOCIOLOGICAL ASSOCIATION

The Rose Monograph Series was established in 1968 in honor of the distinguished sociologists Arnold and Caroline Rose whose bequest makes the Series possible. The sole criterion for publication in the Series is that a manuscript contribute to knowledge in the discipline of sociology in a systematic and substantial manner. All areas of the discipline and all established and promising modes of inquiry are equally eligible for consideration. The Rose Monograph Series is an official publication of the American Sociological Association.

Editor: Teresa A. Sullivan

Editorial Board

The Editor and Editorial Board gratefully acknowledge the contribution of John Butler, The University of Texas at Austin, and Sam Marullo, Georgetown University, as expert reviewers of this manuscript.

BUYING FOR ARMAGEDDON

Business, Society, and
Military Spending Since the
Cuban Missile Crisis

JOHN L. BOIES

RUTGERS UNIVERSITY PRESS
New Brunswick, New Jersey

CONTENTS

LIST OF FIGURES

LIST OF TABLES

ACKNOWLEDGMENTS

MY THANKS TO ALL the people that made this book possible. I give great appreciation to the people at the Library of Congress for their assistance in finding a source for my data. Jeff Paige, Howard Kimeldorf, Mayer Zald, and Thomas Weisskopf all deserve very special thanks for their support, comments, and most especially their patience. My friends all contributed more than they can imagine to this document. Marcene, Jane, Larry, Marc, Pat, Debbie, Vic, Celeste, Misagh, Clarence, Polly, Nelson, and Marg all made life possible over the last few years. My parents and sister Sharon hold a central place in all this because they have been the most patient of all. Mark Fossett and Harland Prechel offered many valuable comments and criticisms. Laurie R. Silver, who stuck with me throughout the process of making this book, deserves special thanks for her support, comments, and love.

BUYING FOR ARMAGEDDON

1

RESEARCH ON THE U.S. MILITARY

THE MILITARY IS A central institution in contemporary industrialized societies. Since World War II the military forces of the more
developed nations have come to represent at once a force that threat-
ens the destruction of contemporary society and perhaps most advanced forms of life on our planet and an organization that is at the
core of western industrialized society and the modern state.[1] Since
World War II the U.S. military has monopolized between 25 and 65
percent of the scientific and engineering talent in the United States
and has absorbed more than 50 percent of total federal government
expenditures (Lens 1970; DeGrasse 1983). Historically, the military
has been the center of state power and is considered by many scholars to be the primal institution of the modern capitalist state (Jacoby
1973; Tilly 1975).

Beyond its importance as one of the linchpins of contemporary
capitalist society, the military is of interest because of the major transformations this enormous organization has undergone. Since World
War II the United States military has increased its technological so-
phistication and destructive power dramatically. More importantly,
perhaps, the commitment of state resources has varied a great deal.
For example, from 1946 to 1955 the proportion of gross national
product (GNP) expended on the armed forces in the United States
ranged from considerably less than 6 percent (about 60 billion 1983
dollars) in 1947 to almost 14 percent in 1955 (nearly 200 billion 1983
dollars, DeGrasse 1983:19–20). More recently, in the late 1970s and
early 1980s the United States underwent one of the most massive

military buildups the world has ever seen. Concomitant with this remarkable expansion of the military came a slew of military engagements including invasions of Panama and Grenada, and air attacks on Libya. The militarily successful defeat of Iraq's occupation forces in Kuwait in 1991 was the largest exercise of this vast arm of the state since the Vietnam war. Most recently, the U.S. military saw action in Somalia, albeit on a humanitarian mission. Even with the change in leadership in the white house in 1993, there are still rumblings of the United States exercising its military might to halt the war in the post-Yugoslavian republics. Despite the collapse of the cold war we still support and use a massive military machine with the apparent hopes (at least in some circles) of limiting the world to just one superpower, the United States (U.S. Office of the Secretary of Defense 1992).[2]

As a framework for analysis, my theoretical focus is on extant theories of the state. In this context I appraise some of the central theories concerning the capitalist state using data on United States military purchases. I also make a first attempt at describing and explaining the types and amounts of military equipment the United States buys. Most contemporary research only reports fluctuations in resource commitment. The role of business in state policymaking is a fiercely debated issue among scholars of the state and military policy (Hooks 1990a; Whitt 1979, 1980, 1982; Domhoff 1970, 1983, 1990; Stubbing and Mendel 1986; Quadagno 1984; Skocpol 1980; Zald and Berg 1978; Barnet 1971; Baran and Sweezy 1966; Rosen 1973; Dahl 1961). Consequently, this research pays special attention to the influence of big business and wealthy individuals on military purchasing.

The many debates and unanswered questions endemic to contemporary studies of the state form the analytic structure of this study. The debates most central to the research I describe here are the conflict between Marxist-instrumentalists and Marxist-structuralists over the level of autonomy the state has vis-à-vis business and the upper class; the question of whether the state represents the interests of business and the upper class as the Marxists and elite theorists suggest, or a large number of diverse competing interests as the pluralists posit; how the policies adopted by the state are affected by the inter- and intraclass conflicts intrinsic to a capitalist society; and the role organizational politics, electoral politics, and other propositions stemming from the Weberian paradigm play in state policymaking.

These questions guide this time series analysis of the distribution, since 1962, of the United States military procurement budget across several functional categories of weapons and other procurement items. The independent variables include measures of domestic political economy, international political economy, business and non-business social movements, and institutional politics. I also include in my analysis time series data on aggregate military procurement, operations and maintenance, and research and development expenditures. The main purposes of this chapter are to provide a general survey of the nature of the literature concerning the military and a discussion of the theory that guides this research.

Sociology, Theories of the State, and the Military

The importance of the armed forces to society has engendered an extensive literature from many disciplines. However, except for considerable work on its organization and culture—of that, the work of Stouffer et al. (1949a, 1949b), *The American Soldier* and of Janowitz, e.g., *The Professional Soldier: A Social and Political Portrait* (1974) and *Military Conflict: Essays in the Institutional Analysis of War and Peace* (1964) are perhaps the most well known—sociology has generally been silent in explaining military phenomena (Shaw 1984; Harries-Jenkins and Moscos, Jr. 1981; Lang 1972). Surprisingly, even the literature on theories of the state, where one would expect considerable attention to be paid to the armed forces, has taken little interest in military policy. Instead, the study of the military state has taken a back seat to the study of the welfare state (Mann 1984; see for examples Quadagno 1984; Skocpol and Orloff 1984; Skocpol 1980).

Some notable exceptions to this trend include James O'Connor's extensive discussion of the military-industrial complex in his book *The Fiscal Crisis of the State* (1973); Baran and Sweezy's (1966) account of the role the military plays in the monopoly capital conditions of late capitalism; and Griffin, Devine, and Wallace's quantitative analysis of the effects of unemployment rates, welfare expenditures, monopoly sector profits, national electoral politics, and other macro-social variables on U.S. military expenditures since World War II (Griffin, Devine, and Wallace 1982a, 1982b). Griffin and his colleagues derive their primary hypotheses from Baran and Sweezy's earlier research. The most recent additions to this short list of literature include Gregory Hooks's (1991, 1990a) work examining the role of the military in post–World War II industrial planning and development and Mac-Dougall's research looking at the effect anti-nuclear and anti-MX social movement organizations have had on the voting behavior of several members of Congress (MacDougall 1990, 1991). This dearth of literature in sociology is remarkable considering the importance of C. Wright Mills's discussion of the ascendancy of the military in U.S. society in *The Power Elite* to the development of research on the military-industrial complex, one of the major strains of research and theory concerning the military (Moskos 1974).

Sociology's inattention to the military is more remarkable considering the resources our society has devoted to national security compared with other public goods. Since World War II the absorption of resources by the U.S. military has always been a larger proportion of the U.S. gross national product than the proportion committed to traditional on-budget welfare programs by the federal government. Figure 1.1 shows that only in the late 1960s did expenditures for welfare (for these charts welfare expenditures include non-trust fund expenditures like Aid to Families with Dependent Children, food stamps, school lunch programs, Office of Economic Opportunity, etc.) begin to approach the resource commitment enjoyed by the organs of national security.[3] However, the 1980s saw welfare's share of resources begin to decline precipitously and the military's share to rise. One should also note that even during the Vietnam war, the nation's commitment to national security as share of GNP never reached the levels of the Korean war and period immediately thereafter.

The degree of historical commitment to national security relative to social welfare by the U.S. federal government is made very clear in figure 1.2. Since 1948 national security and national security–related interest on the debt has absorbed some 57 percent of state resources (based on the assumption that the share of the U.S. debt resulting

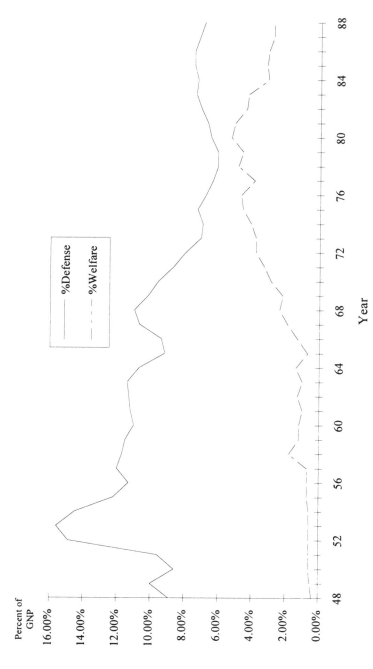

Figure 1.1. Percent of GNP Expended by the U.S. Federal Government on National Security and Welfare Excluding Social Insurance

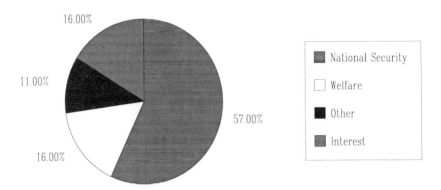

Figure 1.2. Aggregated Percent of Expenditures by the U.S. Government on National Security, Welfare, Interest on Debt, and Other Categories Excluding Off-Budget Expenditures for 1948–1988

from security expenditures is equivalent to the share of on-budget expenditures devoted to national security).

Considering the magnitude of resources committed to national security since World War II, sociology's preeminent concentration on the welfare state has left a major part of the modern state woefully understudied. While the work of sociologists on military organization has contributed much to our understanding of some important aspects of the military, there is still much important research to be done. Moreover, the relative transparency of the linkages among the military, and both the instrumental interests of capital and macrosocial factors (e.g., military competition and policing world capitalism), especially when compared with the welfare system, indicate the military to be an excellent candidate for research on theories of the state.

The majority of studies from other social sciences, such as history, political science, and economics, have concentrated on description or criticism of military policy. Few works present explicit theoretical explanations of military phenomena. Essentially, scholars from these fields have focused on descriptive case studies of decisionmaking and weapons development (e.g., Betts 1981; Ball 1980; Gray 1979; Beard 1976; Greenwood 1975; Tamman 1973; Halperin 1972; Armacost 1969; Bobrow 1969); analytical accounts of the economics and organization of procurement processes (e.g., Gansler 1989, 1980; Kennedy 1983, 1975; Koistinen 1980; Lucas and Dawson 1974); examinations of the economic effects of military expenditures (e.g., DeGrasse 1983; Ball and Leitenberg 1983; Chester 1978); discussions of why arms control has failed (Joseph and Rosenblum 1984; Thee 1978; Art 1974a); and the military-industrial complex literature that has tended to be more polemical and based primarily on anecdotal and journalistic evidence (e.g., Aldridge 1983; Durie and Edwards 1982; Gervasi 1981; Cannizzo 1980; Heise 1979; Bonds 1983; Melman 1970; Kaufman 1972; Barnet 1971; Yarmolinsky 1971).

Although these polemical and policy-oriented studies have dominated the literature, quantitative and qualitative analyses attempting to develop theories of weapons acquisition and military policy are not uncommon. Much of this part of the field has concentrated on aggregate military expenditures or on the proportion of the GNP spent on the military as affected by general economic, political, and social structural variables such as national elections, war, expenditures on social welfare, and unemployment rates (Nincic and Cusock 1979; Clayton 1976); by other nation's military expenditures (Majeski 1983, 1982; Ostrom 1977; Hamblin et al. 1977; Hollist 1977; Lambelet 1975; Moll and Luebbert 1980; Chatterjee 1974) (by far the most extensive literature); and by bureaucratic politics as measured by previous years' budgets (Ostrom 1977).

Two other important bodies of research that attempt to develop explanations of defense policy examine the relationship between the defense interests of members of Congress, measured by military expenditures and defense-related employment in their districts or states, and their voting records on defense bills (e.g., Mayer 1991; Dennis 1978; Cobb 1976, 1973; Grey and Gregory 1968), and between bureaucracy and military policy. The latter category includes studies of the effects of organizational structure and micropolitics (Cuff 1978; Art 1974b; Crecine 1970); budgetary processes (Korb 1981, 1971; Burt 1974/5; Kanter 1975; Stromberg 1979); and organizational competition, especially interservice rivalries on weapons acquisitions (Lucas and Dawson 1974; Huntington 1961).[4]

Although the existing research on defense expenditures and procurement is extensive, it does not provide much explicit insight into the major theoretical questions of concern to this research project.

7

Moreover, there are a number of problems associated with this literature that indicate a need for more research and for research of a somewhat different kind. For example, Gansler, in *The Defense Industry* (1980), describes in great detail the oligopolistic structure of the defense industry and resulting supply and quality problems, but he says little about why this situation exists or persists. This criticism also applies to the extensive case study literature on weapons acquisition decisions. This research provides much interesting detail about who said and did what concerning important government weapons deployment and purchasing decisions and about the micropolitics of organizational decisionmaking, but gives little insight into the larger social and political processes at work shaping weapons acquisition decisions. Furthermore, the case study literature concentrates largely on why the Pentagon decided to buy one particular weapons system rather than another similar system. Neither the case studies nor the economic policy analyses that I have read have extensively discussed the influence of business interests, or of the structure of advanced capitalist economies on weapons decisions.

The more general literature on how organizational factors influence defense policy and weapons acquisitions, which overlaps or builds on much of the case study literature, often attempts to explain why the United States buys the weapons it does. However, this research suffers from some of the same faults as the more specific case studies. This body of research pays little attention to macro processes or the effects of private enterprise on procurement decisions.

A contrast to the work on policy-related and organizational issues is the more polemical portion of the literature on defense outlays and procurement, e.g., Melman's *Pentagon Capitalism* (1970) or Barnet's *Roots of War* (1971).[5] The emphasis of this body of literature is on studying the set of organizations, institutions, systems of interests, and special relationships between key actors in defense policymaking and production. These scholars often portray the military-industrial complex as the most powerful organ of the state and as a significant malevolent force in contemporary society. These works often provide some explicit explanatory theory (usually a combination of state capitalism and crude, but sometimes remarkably accurate, Marxist instrumentalist theory), but rarely present analyses as sophisticated as those that exist in other areas of research. Most of this research is more journalistic than scholarly in nature.

Despite these criticisms, the scholarship examining the military-industrial complex has contributed much of importance to the study of the military in the United States. The major contributions of this body of research include the concept of the permanent war economy (Melman 1970), the idea that the military is possibly the largest and most powerful institution in our society (Yarmolinsky 1971; Melman 1970), the remarkable linkages between the military and private enterprise (Stubbing and Mendel 1986; Barnet 1971; Melman 1970; see Horowitz 1969), and much about the political economic processes influencing military purchases, military policy, and many aspects of foreign policy (Stubbing and Mendel 1986; Gervasi 1981; Yarmolinsky 1972; Barnet 1971; Melman 1970; Pursell 1972; Lapp 1970). A primary precursor to this large literature is C. Wright Mills's work, *The Power Elite* (1956), that details much of the basic theory that has guided military-industrial complex researchers (Moskos 1974). Unfortunately, this strand of research has languished with only a few researchers making new contributions despite its popularity during the late 1960s and into the early 1970s.[6]

The research focusing on quantitative analyses of defense expenditures, although better grounded in theories that explain how large scale social processes influence the amount of money spent on the military (e.g., Griffin, Devine, and Wallace 1982a, 1982b; Nincic and Cusock 1979), is unable to provide much insight into the mechanisms through which these macro processes cause changes in military policy. Moreover, despite the availability, apparent interpretability, and reliability of this type of data (at least for the United States), several characteristics limit its value to the scholar wishing a detailed insight into military policymaking. One problem that limits the usefulness of highly aggregated military expenditure data is that variation in total expenditures on defense across time is narrow except in times of major war (Lieberson, 1971). Over 50 percent of the defense budget is spent on salaries, benefits, pensions, and maintenance, expenditures which are not really controllable by decisionmakers, except over the long term (Reich, 1978). Finally, the aggregate budget provides little information about what the military is buying and thus about what activities the military is capable of performing and what particular interests (organizational, individual, or corporate) are benefiting from military expenditures.

This study fills some gaps in the literature just reviewed. My research provides a systematic sociological study of defense policy using theories of the state and a serious assessment of the amount and kind of influence business has on military policy. Because it examines detailed procurement categories, this research furnishes an appraisal of U.S. military purchases that bridges at least some of the gap between the highly quantitative analyses of aggregated military expenditures and the qualitative case studies of individual weapons systems so common in the literature on military procurement. Unlike other research on the military, the central concern of this study is not just the exploration of factors influencing the levels of military expenditures, but also the distribution of those expenditures between different types of procurement items. The richly textured data used by this study allow the historical record of whole classes of weapons systems decisions to be laid bare to quantitative analysis.

Analytical Framework and Questions

The many questions left unanswered in the increasingly extensive literature on theories of the state provide the theoretical springboard for my analysis of military policy. One central debate focuses on the degree of autonomy the state has vis-à-vis the capitalist class or big business. Marxist-structuralists see the state as performing functions that help reproduce capital, but that are not necessarily in the interests of specific capitalists nor performed at the behest of individuals or groups of capital (Offe and Ronge 1982; Block 1977b; Miliband 1977; Gold, Lo, and Wright 1975). Marxist-instrumentalists and class-dialectical theorists see the state as either a permanent tool of individual and group capitalist interests or as a focus of class conflict with capitalists usually dominating the policy outcomes of the state (Domhoff 1991, 1983; Whitt 1980; Gold, Lo, and Wright 1975).

What is the role of inter- and intraclass conflict on state policy output? Growing out of the debate between the Marxist structural-ists and the Marxist instrumentalists are theories centering on the effects of class dialectics and struggle on the state. Some theorists concentrate on the effects of competing interests among the capitalist class, such as the conflicts between "southern rim" capitalists (the often called "cowboy" capitalists represented by Ronald Reagan) and the traditional "eastern establishment" capitalists (Himmelstein and Clawson 1984; Shoup 1980; Sale 1976) and the conflicts between competing industrial groups and market-related class factions (Whitt 1980). A second, and to some extent competing, group of theorists concentrates on interclass struggle and how it influences the state, particularly in areas concerning domestic social policies (Esping-Anderson, Friedland, and Wright 1979).

What social group or whose interests does the state represent? The central debate here is whether the state essentially serves the inter-ests of business as the Marxists or elite theorists posit (Domhoff 1983, 1970; Alford 1975; Mills 1956) or the competing interests of many different groups as the pluralists suggest (Wildavsky 1979; Zald and Berg 1978; Dahl 1961). The most recent addition to this debate is the work of the modern day state autonomy theorists who posit that the state pursues its own agenda with a great deal of autonomy from the machinations of either the working class or the upper class (e.g., Hooks 1991, 1990; Weir, Orloff, and Skocpol 1988; Skocpol and Orloff 1984; Skocpol 1984). Most of this research focuses on the develop-ment of the welfare state, especially New Deal legislation. Hooks (1990a), however, moves away from this tradition with his study of the development of the post–World War II warfare state.

What are the relative merits of various theoretical propositions concerning policy output stemming from the Weberian paradigm? Although these propositions, until the 1980s, were often ignored in many of the debates among pluralists, elite theorists,[7] and Marxists, they represent a significant body of literature, perhaps even a pre-ponderance of the literature, dealing with the military. The theoreti-cal contentions of this paradigm imply that the characteristics of military purchases are the result of national electoral politics (Griffin, Devine, and Wallace 1982a; Skocpol 1980; Nincic and Cusock 1979); organizational competition and politics (Ostrom 1977; Kanter 1975; Lucas and Dawson 1974); and organizational structure, i.e., bureaucratic rules and regulations (Korb 1981; Gansler 1980) The works of contemporary state-centered theorists such as Skocpol, Orloff, and Hooks are often placed in the Weberian tradition, but their research appears mostly to critique the traditional Marxists (see the Introduction to Weir, Orloff, and Skocpol 1988; and Hooks 1991).

I follow the lead developed by Boris Frankel (1979) in grouping these theory questions into an easily comprehensible order. Frankel classifies research and theory concerning state policymaking of all types into two broad groups, theories positing the relative autonomy of the state from the deliberate political activities of outside domestic groups (theories positing forces endogenous to the state as the primary determinants of state behavior) and theories positing that the state is dependent on outside domestic groups for policy direction (theories positing forces exogenous to the state as the primary determinants of state behavior). The research of the state politics and state-centered theorists and some Marxist-structuralists posit a state that is largely autonomous from outside political action. The state politics and state-centered theorists see the state as essentially unaffected by not only the political machinations of groups outside the state, but, except in extreme circumstance, by most other aspects of the larger society. Marxist structuralists, on the other hand, see the state as largely autonomous from the political processes of much of society; they posit that the state is dependent on society and in charge of reproducing the society. The research derived from the Marxist-instrumentalist perspective obviously proposes a state totally dependent on the capitalist class for its policy direction. In simplified form figure 1.3 diagrams the general relationships that I focus on in the research presented in this book.

The exogenous forces that I examine in this study include the traditional variables examined by the existing literature on the military, monopoly sector economic health (Griffin, Devine, and Wallace 1982a, 1982b; Baran and Sweezy 1966) and defense contractor profitability, a core proposition of the military-industrial complex literature (Stubbing and Mendel 1986; Melman 1970). Additionally, I look at two new exogenous forces not yet empirically tested by the existing literature: the role of elite social movements in defense policymaking, in this case, the New Right social movement measured by the social movement organization most active in foreign and military

Exogenous Forces   **Endogenous Forces**

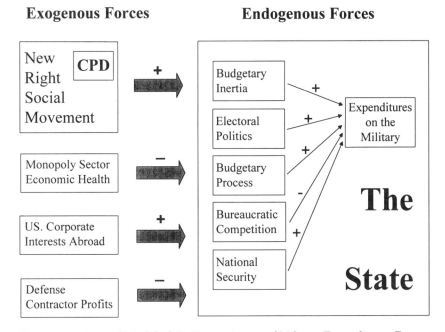

Figure 1.3. General Model of the Determinants of Military Expenditures Examined in This Research Project

policy during the late 1970s and 1980s, the Committee on the Present Danger (CPD); and the role the overseas interests of monopoly capital firms play in determining defense policy. Although most literature examining the military has ignored the importance of overseas corporate interests to policymaking, this phenomenon figures prominently in the work of Baran and Sweezy (1966) and James O'Connor (1973).

The endogenous forces I examine in this book I derived from the existing state politics models of military budgeting and weapons decisions. Central to this body of work is the role of budgetary inertia (Wildavsky 1979). Of great importance to recent sociological ventures in this area is the role of national security in defense decisions (Hooks 1991, 1990a). The way the literature describes this concept, plus the other theoretical components of the state-centered approach, suggest that the empirical manifestation of national security interests will be similar to budgetary inertia (see chapter 4 for a more detailed discussion). In order of declining importance to the state politics model of military expenditures are the potential influence of bureaucratic competition, the structure of the budgetary processes, and electoral politics.

The theoretical propositions shown in figure 1.3 and outlined above drive the selection and organization of both the independent and dependent variables used for this analysis. I must note, however, that the complexity of the literature concerning the military and of the military organizations themselves makes it impossible to fully test the various hypothetical contentions available to date. Instead, the data are used to explore and explicate the processes of U.S. military procurement in light of this body of theory and research

Data and Method

A unique aspect of this project is its use of disaggregated measures of military procurement. The critical data for the study consists of three aggregated measures of military expenditures from *The Statistical Abstract of the United States* and other sources, and twenty-two disaggregated measures of military procurement expenditures from *Prime Military Contract Awards by Service Category and Federal Supply Classification*. The aggregate measures cover the years 1947 to 1986 and the disaggregated time series, with one exception, are for the years 1962 through 1986. For reasons of consistency, however, the research I report in this book concentrates on the data from 1962 to 1986 for all of these measures. The aggregate measures I use have previously appeared in various forms in many published studies such as the work of Griffin, Devine, and Wallace (1982a, 1982b), Nincic and Cusock (1979), Domke, Eichenberg, and Kelleher (1983), and Ostrom (1978). Until now, although the disaggregated data has been available through the Defense Technical Information Service,[8] no social scientist has used any of these data in a quantitative analysis of military procurement. Consequently, the research described here represents only a first attempt at looking at this type of data and, therefore, is more exploratory than confirmatory in nature. Nonetheless, the data I report can support some significant conclusions about the forces behind U.S. military policy.

The lack of extant research using the available disaggregated data is puzzling because so much can be done with data of this type. The central concern of current research using aggregated data has been to examine the fortitude of the state's (and society's) commitment to national security. This concern most often manifests itself in researching the changes in expenditure level from year to year or examining annual changes in the percent of the GNP spent on the military. For questions concerning the kinds of weapons purchased and, therefore, the types of foreign and military policies the military is equipped to support, researchers have turned to case studies and narratives. The disaggregated expenditure data I use here splits procurement expenditures into twelve major categories of weapons.[9] Thus, I can answer questions previously only examined using case studies as well as examining the factors other time-series researchers have addressed. My research looks both at forces influencing the United States' commitment to national security and at factors influencing some aspects of the purposes of the U.S. military machine.

I collected data for twelve major categories and ten sub-categories of procurement. To simplify the data presentation and analysis, I focused my efforts on only nine of the twelve major procurement categories. These groups, however, account for the majority of military procurement and include the classes of expenditures most related to major weapons systems and important types of supplies.[10] Additionally, this study examines three readily available aggregate measures of expenditures. From the many indicators I collected for this project I chose twenty-two variables that best measured the concepts specified as important influences on military procurement decisions by the extant literature. I used ordinary least squares regression to analyze the data for these selected independent and dependent measures. Chapter 5 provides data sources, detailed descriptive statistics for these data, and more explanation of my method.

The measures of procurement expenditures I use in this research are:

1. Expenditures for weapons including small arms, artillery, naval cannon, antiaircraft guns, chemical and biological weapons.
2. Expenditures for ammunition and explosives including gravity bombs, small arms ammunition, artillery and cannon shells, depth charges, mines, and demolition explosives.
3. Expenditures for guided missiles including all the missile components exclusive of warheads for inter-continental ballistic missiles (ICBMs), intermediate-range ballistic missiles, cruise missiles, anti-tank and anti-aircraft missiles, ship-to-ship and anti-submarine missiles.
4. Expenditures for aircraft including airframes, engines, and electronics for transport, bomber, fighter, reconnaissance, attack, and rotary wing aircraft.
5. Expenditures for ships including aircraft carriers, transport vessels, submarines, destroyers, cruisers, minesweepers, barges, and all other types of vessels.
6. Expenditures for communications including radio, telephone, and all other types of communications equipment not a permanent part of a weapons system. Not included in this category are expenditures on power systems, cables, wires, telephone poles, and other miscellaneous equipment.
7. Expenditures for electrical and electronic equipment including night vision equipment, telephone poles and miscellaneous electrical supplies, power sources, switching equipment, small electronic parts and replacements, and non-communication related equipment.
8. Expenditures for armored vehicles including tanks, armored personnel carriers, and mobile artillery vehicles.
9. Expenditures for chemicals including herbicides (such as Agent Orange) and pesticides, paints, solvents, deicing materials, explosives and detonation devices, cleaning compounds, and miscellaneous chemicals, but not including fuels and lubricants.[11]

10. Expenditures for research, development, testing and evaluation (RDT&E) including weapons prototype testing, basic research, grants to corporations for research and development, weapons specifications, the development of weapons modifications, safety testing, and many smaller related types of expenditures.
11. Expenditures for operations and maintenance (O&M) including maintenance of bases and hardware, and all types of naval, aerial, and land-based operations including day-to-day activities, training programs, and military missions.
12. Expenditures for total procurement including all services, supplies, goods, weapons systems, and components. I use the series prepared by the Department of Defense for its various publications.

For the analyses presented in this book these data are converted from current dollars to constant 1972 dollars. Graphs showing the distribution of each category and sub-category in constant 1972 dollars are in Appendix A.

These graphs of expenditures show some interesting and remarkable trends in military procurement. In the majority of the time plots a decided U shape is present with peaks in expenditures during 1962–1969 and during 1982–1984. For most of the variables the middle 1970s show the lowest level of inflation corrected expenditures. This picture of the data contradicts the widely held notion that military expenditures, particularly procurement expenditures, normally show a steady upward trend throughout most of the post–World War II period, with exceptional growth occurring only in times of war (Sivard 1982). For most categories of expenditures a decided down trend in expenditures appears toward the close of our direct involvement in the Vietnam war. This down trend usually ends during the second or third year of the Carter administration. This phenomenon suggests that large scale structural processes are at work influencing the expenditure levels in many of the categories of procurement. The Vietnam war is the obvious candidate for the first peaks in expenditures. The likely cause of the hump in so many categories beginning in the late 1970s is not so obvious.

The Vietnam war, however, does not affect all categories of procurement in the same way, even those categories that show peaks during the war. While the effects of the war appear to be extreme for several categories of procurement, especially ammunition, the effects are not so dramatic for others, especially ships.

The second period of rising expenditures, the late 1970s and the mid-1980s, shows more complexity. Some types of procurement items show high peaks during the Vietnam war but never rise significantly again. This dynamic is especially obvious in the cases of ammunition and chemicals and chemical products.[12] The ships category seems to show a steady growth over the entire time series, but with large fluctuations from year to year. Other procurement categories such as aircraft and electronic equipment show unambiguous rises beginning in 1977–1978.

Some authors suggest that some presidential administrations, e.g., the Carter administration, were committed to low levels of defense spending. Because of the nature of their class constituencies, other administrations, such as Ronald Reagan's, were oriented to higher weapons expenditures (Himmelstein and Clawson 1984; Shoup 1980; Sale 1976;). The data illustrated in these graphs indicate that the beginning of the "largest peacetime buildup the world has ever seen" began not during the Reagan years, but during Jimmy Carter's term in office. This indicates that much more was going on during this period than simple presidential politics.

A final important observation concerning the disaggregated time series is that expenditures on most weapons categories and subcategories show declining expenditures during the period 1984–1986. In almost every case these declines appear after at least 5–7 years of increasing expenditures. Moreover, these declines occur in categories of major equipment like ships, tanks, and communications. Steadily increasing expenditures, however, continue for guided missiles. The complexities manifested in these time plots indicate some of the value of using disaggregated data over the traditional approach. During the period 1962 to 1986, while there are some general consistencies for many types of procurement, other categories differ markedly. The point of this research is to search for the causes both of the consistencies and of the differences in these data.

Chapter Description

In this book I motivate my selection of independent variables in three chapters presenting relevant literature and two case studies that detail processes germane to the problem at hand. The first two chapters deal exclusively with state dependent models of military expenditure decisionmaking. Chapter 2 presents data from a number of qualitative studies that point to defense contractor profits as being an important determinant of the allocation of military expenditures. The next chapter describes a social movement organization that was a core organization of the New Right social movement, The Committee on the Present Danger, as an indicator of outside group political action directed towards influencing defense policy. Chapter 4 lays out the relevant work proposing that the state is relatively autonomous from the specific action of outsiders. This chapter examines two theoretical perspectives, the state politics models[13] and Marxist models. Because most of the important quantitative research by sociologists and political scientists has been done using these perspectives, this chapter proposes variables which, for the most part, have already been extensively examined by other authors.

A superficial examination of the trends in military procurement since 1962 indicates that disaggregating military procurement expenditures uncovers additional layers of information and complexity. This greater detail adds to our knowledge of arms purchases, but also adds dramatically to the job of data analysis. The return on this effort, however, is high because these data provide considerably more insight into the workings of U.S. military policymaking than previously available. Chapter 5 examines these dependent variables, presents descriptive information on the data used here, and describes important methodological considerations. Because the data analysis is relatively complex and required a large number of separate steps, this chapter only presents and discusses the best results of a large body of analyses. Chapter 6 includes my conclusions and the theoretical implications of my findings for sociological theories of the state.

2

**DEFENSE CONTRACTOR POLITICS
AND PROFIT**

Instrumentalism and Research on the Military

MANY RECENT STUDIES exploring the relationship of business to the state document the substantial and disproportionate influence the business community has on the outcomes of public policymaking processes, including those of the legislative, executive, and electoral systems (Ashford 1986; Owens 1986; Domhoff 1983; Chappell 1981; Lydenberg 1980, 1981; Coolidge and Tullock 1980; Silberman and Yochum 1978; Welch 1974, 1976). However, there is a relative paucity of similar research focusing on military policymaking.[1]

There is, however, substantial research on the military, more journalistic and qualitative in nature, that gives numerous examples of where military expenditure decisions were likely to have been heavily influenced by the political action and interests of defense contractors (Kotz 1988; Stubbing and Mendel 1986; Yarmolinsky and Foster 1983; Adams 1981; Barnet 1971; Melman 1970; Yarmolinsky 1971). The bulk of this scholarship goes under the rubric of military-industrial complex theory (see Rosen 1973 for discussion). Much of this work concentrates on the special interest political activities of defense firms and their receipt of special favors from the state (e.g., Stubbing and Mendel 1986; Adams 1981). Although recent sociologists have not made many significant contributions to this literature, it was a sociologist, C. Wright Mills (1956), who provided some of the seminal ideas to this body of theory and research. His discussions of the special political and economic relationships defense contractors have forged with the military in *The Power Elite* served as much of the basis for much of the later research exploring the concept of the military-industrial complex (Moskos 1974).

The corpus of the military-industrial complex literature focuses on the value of defense contracts to defense contractors and the mechanisms that maintain and increase the flow of contracts to their own firms and occasionally to the competition. The majority of this body of literature concludes that defense corporations are a powerful group of special interests that is unique in its relationship to the state. For some researchers, such as Seymour Melman (1970), the military and defense contractors have forged a set of remarkable relationships that set them apart as a special institution in contemporary society. The common strand of theory that binds this sometimes disparate material together is an emphasis on demonstrating that the profit requirements of existing defense contractors significantly affect defense procurement decisions. To some authors the quest for profits is but one of several powerful determinants of defense policy (e.g., Yarmolinsky and Foster 1983; Yarmolinsky 1971; Melman 1970) but to others it is the primary determinant (e.g., Kotz 1988; Cannizzo 1980; Ferrell 1972). Another central aspect of this perspective is the common assumption that individual defense firms do all the political activity with only scant organization among competing firms.

The central purpose of this chapter is to explore the diverse and detailed qualitative literature on defense contractor political action to derive a general theoretical thread tying together this body of material. I use this grounded theorizing approach to build a hypothesis testable with available data (see Strauss 1990; Miles 1987 for more on grounded theory techniques). The diversity of the relevant examinations of defense contractor influence and the absence of extant quantitative statistical studies concerning contractor influence makes my detailed review of the literature necessary. Additionally, this fascinating literature provides much information concerning the variegated forces behind the development of a range of U.S. military policies. A review of this literature makes an excellent springboard for a critical study of military procurement.

Among defense contractors and the modern state there exist many special institutional and economic relationships that give defense firms remarkable opportunities to exert influence and power over state decisionmaking. While some of these relationships are unique to the defense industry, e.g., the monopsony market for defense goods,[2] others are also common in many other industries with interests linked to the state, e.g., membership on advisory bodies. The literature emphasizes two ends of the set of special institutional, political, and economic relationships among the military and its private industry suppliers as being especially important to consider. The dependency the Pentagon has on corporations supplying defense materials and services makes the state systematically biased toward the interests of these companies. On the other hand, for many firms supplying defense materials the U.S. military is the only available market for their production. This forces firms to undertake many forms of political enterprise to ensure the future of their profits.

Maintaining the Defense Industry

One important characteristic of the relationship defense firms have with the central state is the high level of concentration present in most parts of the defense industry. In a large number of weapons categories just a few firms provide the vast majority of production. Just eight firms provided 100 percent of all satellites, space boosters, fighter aircraft, and attack aircraft in the late 1960s. Just four firms provided 95 percent or more of missile reentry vehicles, aircraft fire control systems, inertial navigation systems, missile guidance systems, attack aircraft, fighter aircraft, space boosters, and nuclear submarines (U.S. Senate 1968). A few large defense contractors provide the majority of production for several categories of weapons, e.g., General Dynamics makes the majority of fighter aircraft and air-to-air missiles as well as all the submarine-launched ballistic missile (SLBM) submarines (the Trident, for example) procured by the U.S. Department of Defense. Rockwell International produces most of the ballistic missile guidance systems and missile engines. For many products, such as ships' propellers, tank hulls, and aircraft engines, all production has been concentrated in just one or two suppliers since the middle 1960s (Gansler 1989, 1980). Defense analysts concur that defense firm concentration has increased since the late 1960s. About half of six thousand aerospace suppliers left the field from 1967 to 1980 (Gansler 1989).

These high levels of concentration have several important effects on defense decisionmaking. Many firms have become "national assets" because so few firms produce such very important products. Therefore, the state has to protect them from normal economic and social forces (Kaldor 1981; Gansler 1980). This concept heavily influenced U.S. military policymaking during the post–World War II rearmament. The very influential Finletter Commission, for example, concluded in 1948:

> In a freely competitive economy the number of companies manufacturing a particular product levels off at a point determined by the ordinary laws of economics. In the case of aircraft it would be dangerous to rely only on the operations of these laws.

The committee continued by stating:

> Government can and should, however, create an atmosphere as conducive as possible to profitable operations in the aircraft manufacturing business. (Pursell 1972:184–185).[3]

Because the state has few alternative sources for most important defense materials, many firms were given incentives to entice them into defense production, a policy predating most contemporary defense contractors. For example, before the turn of the century U.S. steel companies refused to make armor plate for the Navy. Most U.S. firms at the time did not have production facilities suitable to make the high quality materials the Navy demanded. Also, the exacting quality requirements dissuaded those firms with the appropriate facilities from seeking government contracts. Consequently, the Navy initiated many of the special and lucrative contracting arrangements so common in the industry today to induce the unwilling steel companies to make armor plate. Perhaps the most important of these concessions still in use is guaranteed profit margins (Lischka 1977). Now these special arrangements are sufficiently institutionalized that, despite many attempts at reform, little change has occurred in the way the Pentagon does business (Gansler 1989).

World War II dramatically accelerated the state's increasing dependency on private enterprise for key defense materials and services that began before World War I (Koistinen 1980; Cooling 1979; Melman 1970). The focus on high technology weapons (especially aircraft and nuclear weapons) in the post-war period ensured the continuation of this trend. This increasing dependency has several profound effects on defense policymakers. As Walter Adams wrote in 1968:

> . . . the government becomes almost totally dependent on the chosen instruments, i.e., creatures of its own making, for effectuating public policy. Lacking any viable in-house capabilities, competitive yardsticks, or the potential for institutional competition, the government becomes—in the extreme—subservient to the private and special interests whose entrenched power bears the government seal (58).

An important manifestation of this dependency, deliberate or otherwise, is the phenomenon called the follow-on imperative (Kaldor 1981; Kurth 1978). Because the state views key defense firms, particularly aerospace firms, as national resources, it becomes essential for national security that these firms remain in the business of designing and making weapons. One way the state can assure this is to allocate defense moneys in ways that guarantee at least a minimal but profitable existence for the main prime contractors, their key subsidiaries, and most important subcontractors. Consequently, the military will rapidly provide contracts for a different but similar weapon or for a major modification of an existing weapon when a production run of a major weapon ends (Stubbing and Mendel 1986). Some examples discussed by Kurth (1978) include the following of Lockheed's C-130 transport, first made before 1960, with the C-141 in 1964, the C-5A in 1968, and the C-5B wing modification program of the 1970s. Another example is the Minuteman I and II system, built by Boeing, that was followed on by the Minuteman III. More recently, the Department of Defense funded upgrades to the Minuteman III's warheads—Command, Control, Communications, and Intelligence (C³I)—and added additional Electromagnetic Pulse and blast hardening to the missiles' silos. Important contracts for the MX missile, including the replacement of recently modified Minuteman III missiles with MX missiles, soon followed the previous Minuteman III upgrades.

Kurth's (1978) study of the follow-on imperative found six major aerospace production lines, each dominated by a few aerospace giants: large bombers (Boeing, Rockwell International); fighters and fighter-bombers (General Dynamics, McDonell-Douglas, Grumman); military transports (Lockheed); strategic missiles (Boeing, Lockheed); missile defense systems (McDonell-Douglas, AT&T); and space systems (Grumman, Rockwell-International).

An earlier study by Kurth (1973) describes an additional imperative, the bail-out imperative. According to Kurth, bail-outs are contracts awarded to firms, not because the military has a given hardware need best satisfied by a given firm's product, but because a firm or several firms are suffering financial difficulties, usually unrelated to their defense-oriented business. Thus, hardware is procured based on the economic health of the firm rather than because of defense needs. Kurth found this to have less explanatory value for aerospace procurement in the 1960s than the follow-on imperative, but he was not able to analyze the state's reaction to the economic troubles suffered by defense firms in 1970–1973 (Stubbing and Mendel 1986).

Kurth considers the bail-out imperative as a significant factor behind the C-5B wing modification program given to Lockheed in 1975,[4] the Division Air Defense (Divad) contract to Ford in 1982, and the F-111 contract to General Dynamics in 1962. Stubbing and Mendel (1986) write that because Boeing Corporation does so well in its civilian business, it has lost out to less economically successful firms on many large contracts even though its design and production plans were far superior to its competition, e.g., the F-111, KC-10 tanker, and C-17 transport. Bail-outs of defense firms sometimes come in the form of special loans like Lockheed's 1971 subsidized loan of $250 million and the state guaranteed loans of $1.5 billion to Chrysler Corporation in 1979[5] (Stubbing and Mendel 1986; Barnet and Muller 1974).

To encourage firms to expand into new production the state also commonly provides a large quantity of the necessary capital goods (Hooks 1991; Gansler 1980; Melman 1970). For example, in 1967 General Electric and North American Rockwell (now Rockwell International) each used over $100 million (current dollars) worth of state-owned production equipment. AVCO Corporation used almost $90 million worth of equipment and the fifteen largest holders of state-owned equipment held a total of $2.5 billion in state provided facilities at the end of the 1960s (Melman 1970:79).

The material just reviewed indicates that the Pentagon's significant dependency on private contractors for its war materials has made it necessary for the state to use its considerable economic and political power to maintain a defense industry large enough to supply its peacetime needs as well as to allow at least some possibility of speedy wartime expansion.[6] Indeed the high level of concentration in some defense industry sectors has made it necessary for the state to have an interest in maintaining individual contractors and subcontractors (especially in the areas of shipbuilding, aircraft, and missiles).

To maintain adequate defense industrial capacity the state has forged a unique system of long-term relationships with defense firms that buffers these firms from many of the rigors of the free market. The state also occasionally uses exceptional means like very large loan guarantees and biasing contract awards to ensure that some firms will remain viable. The bottom line of the state's relationship to the defense industry is that if the individual companies cannot produce adequate profit for them to stay in business, then it is up to the state to provide whatever is necessary for the maintenance of adequate profit. The central common hypothesis of this literature is that declines in defense contractors' profitability should cause rises in procurement expenditures to offset the failure of these firms to make money.

Defense Contractor Political Enterprise

The structural conditions of the defense industry certainly stack the cards in the favor of the interests of the largest defense firms. However, despite this systemic state bias favoring the interests of defense contractors, many of these firms undertake numerous deliberate and carefully organized actions to further promote their interests. Many defense firms, especially the largest, are remarkably dependent on the U.S. military for much of their sales. From 1960 to 1967 the average percentage of total sales of contractors with total prime contract awards of $1 billion or more (uncorrected for inflation) was 42 percent. The most dependent firm was Thiokol (a maker of rocket fuels and engines) with 96 percent of its sales coming from defense contracts. The least dependent firms were General Motors and Standard Oil of New Jersey, each with 2 percent (calculated by author from Melman 1970:77–78). Even among companies doing only a limited amount of military production, such as General Motors and Chrysler, defense contracts often provide a disproportionate amount of the firms' profits (Stubbing and Mendel 1986; Barnet and Muller 1974). This dependency on a single client for profits puts the defense contractor in the position of having to market its product through political action rather than through normal marketing activities. Hence, the term contractor political enterprise is a good description of how defense companies market their product.

It is reasonable to believe that defense contractors would be willing to devote significant resources to maintaining and expanding their existing markets as do other types of firms like food processing, automobile, and cosmetic firms. *Advertising Age* calculated that the average U.S. firm in the period from 1960 to 1973 spent about 10 percent of its sales on advertising (Barnet and Muller 1974). A large defense firm like General Dynamics would have had over $700 million available to influence the state and otherwise promote their interests in 1987 if they budgeted this average proportion to lobbying activities! Although it is unlikely that defense contractors spend this kind of money lobbying the state, even 1 percent of this amount (one-tenth of one percent of sales), $7 million, would make a substantial war chest to bring to Washington.

The tremendous resources that defense firms command enable them to apply very refined, expensive, and long-term programs to further their interests. For example, Rockwell International has undertaken several multi-year efforts, including elaborate letter-writing drives, campaign donations, petition drives, and other activities, to keep the B-1 bomber program alive. One such program had employees of a subsidiary (Admiral) send letters to selected congressional representatives to disguise the originator of the lobbying efforts (Kotz 1988). Lockheed printed and sent (providing separate stamps for the enclosed letters) packets containing individually tailored letters with no indication of Lockheed involvement to its employees and retirees. Nearly one hundred thousand employees and retirees received packets, forty thousand of whom returned postcards acknowledging that they had forwarded their letters to their Congressional representatives (Thompson 1986). Along with letter-writing programs defense contractor lobbying campaigns have many other tools available including political action committees (PACs) and Congressional honoraria. For example, Common Cause noted that the top five contractors in their respective states contributed $7.9 million to the members of the House and Senate Armed Services Committees (Common Cause 1989).

Advisory Councils and Committees

One of the many important tools used by defense firms for influencing the state is representation on advisory councils and committees that advise federal bureaucracies and Congressional organizations. Since at least the Whisky Rebellion of 1794, committees composed of private citizens have been created to advise Presidents, Congressional committees, and federal bureaucracies (Morehead 1975). However, it was not until World War II that the number of advisory boards, committees, and councils reached contemporary levels. The war production board alone was responsible for over seven thousand industry advisory councils (McConnell 1966). The Annual Report of the President (1981) listed over one thousand advisory committees and boards connected to the executive branch in 1980.

The membership of these committees usually consists of private citizens from business, academe, and nonprofit organizations (Priest,

Sylves, and Scudder 1984). Mills (1956) and Domhoff (1978) describe advisory committees as business-dominated and as important ways businesses present their special interests to state managers. Therefore, it is not surprising that the federal agencies with the greatest business representation on their advisory councils and boards are the Departments of State, Defense, Commerce, and Interior (Useem 1979). McQuaid (1976), Roose (1975), Steck (1975), and McConnell (1966) conclude that business significantly influences federal policies because of its participation in these committees.

For defense contractors, representation on advisory committees assisting in developing defense policies is an important part of their business operations. Top-level managers from defense firms represent the interests of these firms by actively participating in potentially influential advisory councils and committees. An excellent contemporary example of the makeup of these councils is the advisory council to the Office of Technology Assessment's (OTA) task force on anti-satellite (ASAT) and ballistic missile defense (BMD) technologies (Office of Technology Assessment 1986).

This OTA advisory council had seventeen members, including Solom Buschsbaum, an executive vice-president of AT&T, George Jeffs, President of Rockwell International, H. Alan Pike of Lockheed, and Seymour Zeiberg of Martin Marietta. AT&T is a major defense contractor that supplies the military with communications equipment, sensing instruments, software, missile electronics, and other hardware related to BMD. This firm was also the prime contractor for the Safeguard anti-ballistic missile (ABM) program of the 1960s. Lockheed makes aircraft and missiles including the Aegis surface-to-air missile (SAM) and the Trident SLBMs. Lockheed is also a major proponent and developer of the "pop-up" submarine launched BMD system. This is one of the several alternative BMD systems explored by the OTA investigators. Martin Marietta provides missile launchers, missile support systems, electronics, and would have received significant contracts if the Department of Defense adopted the ground launched "terminal defense" BMD alternative. Rockwell International is the prime contractor for the space shuttle and the B-1, and supplies missile propulsion systems and aerospace electronic systems. Regardless of what form of BMD system might have been deployed, Rockwell International would have profited handsomely. It is very important to realize, however, that the expenditures on research and demonstration projects relating to SDI provide considerable income to all the firms currently involved in the SDI program.

Other members of the advisory council included representatives from Sandia Labs, Stanford Linear Accelerator, Lawrence Livermore Labs, and the Los Alamos National Laboratory, all organizations receiving the preponderance of research and development (R&D) funds for the strategic defense initiative (SDI). The rest of the committee consisted of four consultants and people from Harvard University, twelfth-highest university recipient of Department of Defense money in 1964 (Pursell 1972), Columbia University, ranked fourth in 1964, and Rockefeller University. Colin S. Gray, one of the foremost ideological proponents of SDI, was also on the committee.

It is uncertain whether the members of this OTA advisory council significantly influenced the outcome of the final report. However, while the conclusions of the report are highly critical of many very important aspects of existing and future BMD and ASAT technologies and policies, the report recommends continued support of existing BMD and ASAT R&D and technology demonstrations. At the time of the OTA study, the proposed funding totaled about $6.6 billion per year through the year 1995.[7] The bulk of the expenditures on SDI research have gone to the firms and organizations represented on the advisory committee (Cushman 1988; Axelrod, Schwartz, and Boies 1986)!

The President's Air Policy Commission, active in 1947 and 1948, is another example of the influence defense firms can have on policymaking by participating in these commissions. Historians and sociologists recognize this commission, most commonly known as the Finletter Commission, as being very influential in shaping U.S. defense policy during the post–World War II rearmament (Yergin 1978; Hooks 1991, 1990b; Pursell 1972; Domhoff 1970). The commission's recommendations centered on a massive buildup of aircraft, an emphasis on high technology weapons—most particularly nuclear weapons—and the importance of the government maintaining a sizable aircraft industry even in times when there is only a limited demand for new airframes (President's Air Policy Commission 1948).

A remarkable feature of the makeup of this commission is the high degree of representation of one defense-oriented aircraft manufacturing firm, Curtiss-Wright. Two of the four advisers to the commission, C. H. Colvin and Grover Loenig, had long histories of directorships, management, and consulting with Curtiss-Wright. The executive director, S. Paul Johnston, was the Washington, D.C. manager of Curtiss-Wright. Of the three members of the commission, one, John A. McCone, was a director of Curtiss-Wright as well as one of the organizers of Bechtel, the largest military construction firm in the world. Additionally, high-level managers of Curtiss-Wright testified before the committee several times. During the tenure of the commission, Curtiss-Wright was suffering severe economic trouble from its failure to secure defense contracts in the immediate post-war period (Bright 1978). Other aircraft firms represented on the commission were American Republic Aviation and Grumman.

The commission's makeup also included prominent businessmen such as Thomas K. Finletter, chair of the commission and George P. Baker, vice chair, a member of the Astor family and very politically active. Member A. D. Whiteside, then president of Dun and Bradstreet, was actively involved with the National Recovery Administration and Business Advisory Council. Other prominent members of the upper class represented on the commission were S. Paul Johnston, Palmer Hoyt, publisher of the *Denver Post*, Grover Loenig, John C. Cooper, vice president of Pan American Airlines, S. W. Morgan of Lehman Brother's and later vice president of American Republic Aviation, and John A. McCone (Burch 1980; Who's Who in America 1950–51). Scholars examining the influence of the very wealthy on public policy in the United States label the wealthy members of this advisory committee corporate liberals (Pursell 1972; Domhoff 1970).

Defense firms exercise at least some significant influence through advisory councils and boards created to assist the Department of Defense and other government bodies. The defense literature has not significantly explored the extent of this influence. Indeed, social scientists of any description have not adequately studied the phenomenon of advisory councils and commissions (Priest et al. 1984).

Industry as the Source of Policy Recommendations

Another very important mechanism for defense contractor influence is the widespread use of defense contractors by the Department of Defense to study and develop military requirements and specifications for future weapons systems. For many types of weapons systems, such as tanks, ballistic missiles, and aircraft, this is particularly common (Adams 1981; Kaldor 1981). Boeing Co., for example, was the prime contractor for the Strat-X study completed in 1969 that produced the original specifications for the MX missile and initiated further interest in a small vehicle-mounted mobile intercontinental ballistic missile (ICBM), now called the Midgetman[8] (Holland 1985; Holland and Hoover 1985). Boeing remains the major subcontractor for the MX and is one of the major competitors for the Midgetman contract (along with Lockheed and Goodyear).

More recently Boeing was the prime contractor for a 1977 study of the ability of U.S. society to survive a nuclear attack, commonly called the Boeing Study (Jones and Thompson 1978). Ostensibly, this project was to examine the effectiveness of civilian defense measures. The most widely publicized results, however, focused on the importance of acquiring the MX missile and the adoption of a hardware intensive warfighting strategic nuclear policy (Jones and Thompson 1978). Cold warriors like Leon Goure and Colin S. Gray and organizations like the Committee on the Present Danger and the American Security Council used the results from this study in their campaigns to block ratification of SALT II. One of the authors of this study, Thomas K. Jones, later became a Reagan administration official and, along with four colleagues, was indicted in April, 1988 for receiving over $485,000 in illegal compensation from Boeing just before taking office (*NYT* 1988).

As one corporate vice president said, "[the government] . . . depends on companies like ours to tell them what they need" (Kaldor 1981:69). A study finished in the early 1970s that reviewed ten major weapons programs found that defense contractors " . . . are profoundly influential in the origination and development of new program ideas. . . . " (Fox 1974:101).

Revolving Door Phenomenon

Most scholars as well as laypeople associate the revolving-door phenomenon with regulatory agencies, but it is equally, if not more, ubiquitous in defense-related bureaucracies and is present even in Congress (Reed 1975). Defense contractors frequently hire retired military officers as vice presidents of public relations, technical consultants, lobbyists, or any of a large number of similar positions (Melman 1970). Employees of defense contractors also end up working for the Department of Defense, Department of State, and in executive branch high-level policy positions. For example, Casper Weinberger and George Schultz were both high-level managers of Bechtel Corporation, the world's largest military construction firm. Thomas K. Jones became Deputy Undersecretary of Defense for Research and Engineering in 1981 after a long stint as Manager of Program and Product Evaluation at the Boeing Co. (Scheer 1982).

The number of retired military officers working for defense contractors rose from 768 in 1959 to 2,072 in 1969 (Yarmolinsky 1971). Despite several pieces of legislation regulating and restricting this practice, by the early 1980s this number reached over three thousand (Stubbing and Mendel 1986). The hiring of ex-government officials by defense contractors has spread beyond the military to include Congress. Some of the better-known Congressional members and staffers that have gone to work as defense firm lobbyists include Thomas Gunn, hired by McDonell-Douglas, John Ford, who works for AVCO Corp., and Clark MacGregor, who heads the Washington office of United Technologies (Stubbing and Mendel 1986).

Ex-employees of the Department of Defense and related bureaucracies represent an enormous store of technical skills relevant to weapons technologies. What is more important for many firms, however, is that these people have important knowledge of the workings of the complex bureaucratic procedures necessary for a weapons system to move from a dream in an engineer's mind to a large contract award. Ex-government employees and officials, especially highly-placed people, also bring a wealth of political and social contacts with them that can mean instant cash for them and instant contracts for their new employers (Stubbing and Mendel 1986; Yarmolinsky and Foster 1983; Melman 1970; Yarmolinsky 1971). For example, Stubbing and Mendel (1986) point to the activities of three retired three star army generals as being instrumental in Ford Motor Co. being awarded the Divad system contract. The Department of Defense awarded the contract despite evidence that Ford and the Army falsified test data and photographs so the system could pass the testing and evaluation phases of the contract award process.

The potential for high-paid employment with a defense contractor after retirement must also have some effect on the behavior of Department of Defense bureaucrats towards these possible employers. Defense firms recruit most of the ex–Department of Defense employees they ultimately hire from the various auditing divisions and sections in the Pentagon and the three services (Reed 1975). It seems possible that a defense contract auditor could feel constrained by prospects of future employment to overlook accounting errors during audits of potential future employers. However, I know of no research that tests this hypothesis.

The movement of defense contractor personnel into temporary government positions appears to be a different phenomenon. Rather than bringing expertise to government that is useful in furthering the goals of the Department of Defense or related organizations, many scholars suggest these people take government positions to ensure that the interests of the ex-employee's firm, industry, or social class are heard (or perhaps prevail) at the highest levels of government (Domhoff 1970, 1983). Two recent examples of this phenomenon include George Schultz and Casper Weinberger, both ex-executives of Bechtel, the world's largest military construction contractor. During the Nixon administration the position of deputy secretary of defense was held by three men, two of whom, David Packard and Kenneth Rush, were executives of major defense contractors—Hewlett-Packard and Union Carbide, respectively (Burch 1980). During the Kennedy administration some of the more prominent appointees with ties to defense contractors included Fred Koth, an ex-director of Textron Inc., as Secretary of the Navy and Robert McNamara, president of Ford Motor Co., as Secretary of Defense (Burch 1980).

Defense Contractor Lobbying Activities

Defense contractors have become extremely adept Congressional lobbyists. Because of their specialized technical knowledge, their army of ex-government officials, and their great wealth, defense firms are able to carry out long-term and apparently successful lobbying campaigns to maintain and increase the flow of contracts. Nick Kotz (1988) in his study of the B-1 bomber outlined several lobbying campaigns organized by Rockwell International and its subsidiaries, including Admiral, that lasted as long as three years and with documented expenses, excluding staff salaries, as high as $115,895.

Defense firms do not limit themselves just to the available legal means of lobbying. These companies also use many traditional, but less legitimate, activities to further their interests including bribery, gift-giving, and wining and dining to help officials come to the proper decisions. Rockwell International, then called North American Rockwell, for example, made illegal campaign contributions to Richard Nixon, sent Pentagon officials on all-expense-paid hunting trips to private preserves, and entertained various Department of Defense people with elaborate Bimini vacations during at least one campaign to promote the B-1 bomber (Kotz 1988). Glenn Martin Co., now Martin Marietta, has also used Caribbean trips as effective political tools (Yarmolinsky 1971).

Wining and dining individual and small groups of bureaucrats and members of Congress at expensive Washington restaurants and hotels is another common form of reward offered by contractors for favorable decisions. Because of Pentagon rules made during the 1960s, indiscreet partying, especially with drugs and prostitutes present, has largely become a thing of the past. However, as one Air Force employee said, "McNamara drove the entertainment underground." Another Pentagon official reported that " . . . the contractors are just a lot more discreet now. . . . " (Yarmolinsky 1971)

A type of targeted benefit that has become very popular in recent years is the paying of substantial honoraria to members of Congress for brief lectures, short junkets to the home office, luncheon meetings, seminars, briefings, and other gatherings (Walsh 1986). Until recently, honoraria to members of Congress for speaking engagements and other special interest group gatherings could amount to 30 percent of a congressperson's salary, although many have received much more than that amount. The law required that any payments beyond the 30 percent limit be given to nonprofit organizations and are presumably tax-deductible. In 1988 the total amount of payments to members of Congress was $1,440,000. Leaders of key committees are the major recipients of this money. Of the $457,387 paid by eleven major defense contractors (nearly one-third of the total honoraria paid by *all* organizations!), $307,387 went to members of the House and Senate Armed Services Committees (*NYT* 1989).

Honoraria are usually part of sophisticated lobbying strategies being undertaken by a major contractor or small group of contractors. For example, in 1983 the Army attempted to put future contracts for the M-1 tank turbine engine up for competitive bidding because AVCO Corporation failed to meet production goals and quality requirements. AVCO successfully used speaking fees and campaign donations to get key Congressional leaders in both the House Defense Appropriations Subcommittee and House Armed Services Committee to bar the Army from seeking competitive bids for the turbine contracts. An important champion for AVCO was Congressman William Chappell (D-Florida) who received $8,000 in speaking fees in 1982. Other members of these committees received thousands of dollars in speaking fees and campaign donations within a few days of the Army's announcement. Representative Dan Daniel (D-Virginia), the recipient of $2,000 in speaking fees, and Representative Addabbo (D-New York), who, until he received $5,000 in campaign donations from AVCO's PAC, was an adamant supporter of competitive bidding for military hardware, cast the swing votes when the committee ultimately rejected the Army's proposal for competitive bidding (Stubbing and Mendel 1986).

Campaign donations are also an integral part of the sophisticated lobbying strategies employed by defense contractors. Members of Congress as well as the President are the focus of this political tool (Kotz 1988; Stubbing and Mendel 1986). While qualitative evidence concerning campaign donations by businesses has long been available—e.g., Rockwell International's illegal donations to the Committee to Re-elect the President during the firm's early attempts to get funding for the B-1 bomber (Kotz 1988)—systematic data was not available. However, significant changes in the late 1960s and 1970s along with the explosive growth in business-sponsored political action committees has made a gold mine of data available on business political activity (Epstein 1980; Seigfried 1980).

Recent research using business-sponsored PAC data for Fortune 500 firms indicates that the most important and consistent predictor of corporate-sponsored political action committee receipts during the 1976 and 1980 election cycles was the total value of defense contracts received by the firm in 1979. For every million dollars in defense contracts a firm received in 1979, PAC receipts increased an average of fifteen dollars in 1976 and sixty-six dollars in 1980. The majority of the extant literature on business political behavior focuses on the size of the firm as the most important determinant of business political activity. However, analyses of PAC receipts show that sales volume has no statistically discernible effect for 1976 PAC receipts. For 1980 receipts, each million dollars in sales increased PAC size by less than one dollar (Boies 1989). For some firms, such as General Dynamics or Rockwell International, over 80 percent of their sales are to the U.S. federal government (Gansler 1980).

A typical defense contractor PAC is the Boeing Political Action Committee (BPAC), sponsored by the Boeing Aerospace Corporation. In the eighteen month period of January, 1987 through June, 1988 BPAC raised $316,931 (typical in size for a top defense contractor) and disbursed $242,235 to 155 House and Senate candidates. Overwhelmingly, the PACs gave money to the incumbents holding seats on committees directly involved in allocating resources for national security, e.g., House and Senate Armed Services Committees, House Appropriations Committee, and House Science and Space Technology Committee. According to the fundraising letter BPAC's management sent to employees the goal of BPAC is to " . . . [maintain] a healthy political and economic environment in which our company operates" (Smith 1988:B-3). The effectiveness of these donations for maintaining a climate good for Boeing's profits is difficult to measure, but Boeing has been able to maintain relatively high profits throughout the 1980s from both its military and civilian businesses.

Recent evidence examining the influence of PAC campaign donations from ten interest groups on Congressional voting across a wide range of legislation indicates that, taken in isolation, PAC donations have but weak effects on Congressional voting behavior (Grenzke 1989). Mayer (1991) specifically examined the relationship between defense corporation PAC donations and Congressional voting behavior and found no significant effects. However, Mayer did not examine the role of PAC contributions as part of larger more complex lobbying endeavors such as Rockwell's campaign to build the B-1 bomber. Grenzke, despite her overall negative findings, found evidence suggesting that PAC contributions were influential, not in themselves, but as part of more complex lobbying endeavors. It is important to note that Mayer, even in his case study of AVCO corporation's efforts to retain sole-source status for M-1 tank engine production, ignored all other types of political activity undertaken by defense firms. The evidence seems to indicate that while PAC contributions by themselves have limited independent impact on Congressional voting, they can be an important part of sophisticated lobbying campaigns. Moreover, since most of what is of interest to defense companies occurs in committee and in the Pentagon bureaucracy long before or even after the floor votes, it is likely that most defense firm political action is oriented toward those points in the political process.[9]

The role that campaign donations play in Congressional decision-making is unclear, although the carefully timed use of PAC donations and honoraria seemed to change the policy of the House regarding competitive bidding on the M-1 gas turbine engines. The research reported here reveals that defense firms routinely bring their interests to the attention of both elected and appointed officials of the state. In many cases it appears that the political actions of these contractors influence government decisions. While the existing research makes it clear that defense contractors pursue their interests through a remarkably wide spectrum of political activities, it does not present a clear picture of the level or type of influence these activities have on defense procurement. In some cases, such as AVCO's campaign surrounding the M-1 tank engine and Rockwell's pursuit of the B-1 bomber, the influence of defense firms is readily apparent. For other cases the picture is less transparent. However,

Mayer (1991) concludes that political action involving campaign donations has only indirect influence on policy by helping to ensure that defense industry supporters get reelected to Congress.

The literature on the political behavior of defense corporations clearly indicates that defense firms have many ways of influencing defense procurement decisions. The literature, however, does not clearly demonstrate just how influential these firms are in determining the outcomes of the defense procurement process. The obvious motivation behind the political action of these firms is the maintenance and enhancement of the profits of the individual defense firms.

Measurement of Military-Industrial Complex Influence

The military-industrial complex approach concentrates on two aspects of the relationship between defense contractors and the state. This literature presents the state as behaving largely in the interests of the businesses receiving the most defense contracts, at least to the extent of maintaining some adequate level of profitability. This approach also holds that defense contractor profits are the central driving force behind the political action undertaken by defense firms. Profits are the most central and identifiable interest affecting defense contractor behavior.

At the core of this perspective is the contention that declining profits spur increases in expenditures by the Pentagon to counteract individual or small groups of contractors' accumulation crises. If this central argument does represent reality, a measure of the profitability of defense firms should make a good predictor of defense contract allocation. Indeed, because some of the literature on the relationship defense firms have with the state suggests the existence of a structural bias in the system of procurement decisionmaking toward ensuring defense firm profitability, a measure of defense firm profitability possibly provides significant insight into the impact the structure of the military-industrial complex has on defense contract allocation. The literature leads me to expect that when the profits of defense firms decline, expenditure levels should increase to maintain

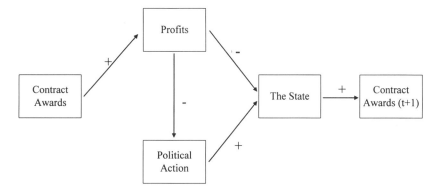

Figure 2.1. Model of Relationship between Contractor Profit and Contract Awards

defense firm profitability. This should happen both because of the built-in institutional biases and because firm political action should increase as companies become more desperate for money. This prediction is very similar to the arguments outlined in several other time-series studies of the effects of the needs of business on state policy outcomes because it places declining profitability as the factor that ultimately spurs the state into doing what it can to stimulate firm profitability (Jacobs 1988; Griffin, Devine, and Wallace 1982a, 1982b).

Figure 2.1 illustrates the relationship described by the literature. When contract awards are high, firm profits are also likely to be high. Firms are likely to feel less pressure to seek out more contracts through political action and the state is likely to have less concern about the profitability of defense companies when making decisions about contract awards. Additionally, low profitability from any source will spur the firm to undertake more political action to pressure the state into granting larger contracts to boost firm profitability. The bias built into the state toward the protection of defense firm profits will increase the weight of defense firm profits in procurement decisions. This should result in an increase in contract awards to the firm or group of firms. The key link I examine in this study is the one between firm profitability and the expenditures on defense contracts.

In this study of the efficacy of business political influence contractor profits I measure contractor profitability with the net earnings per share averaged across the top fifteen defense contractors for 1962–1987. Data are from the U.S. Department of Defense periodical *100 Companies, the Top 100 Companies Receiving Prime Contract Awards from the U.S. Department of Defense* (Annual) and from each firm's annual stockholders reports. Because my measure of defense contractor profitability in this study is only the profits of the top fifteen defense firms, I expect the strongest relationships to be with those categories of weapons produced by these top fifteen firms. Thus, the procurement categories that should be most responsive to the profit margins of this group of contractors are aircraft, ships, guided missiles, electronics, and communications. Although lag times between when Congress decides to appropriate money for a weapon and when the state spends the money vary depending on what type of weapon is being considered—e.g., aircraft carriers and other large weapons might take years between Congressional decision and the first large payment to a contractor—the extant literature indicates that a one-year lag is most appropriate.

3

ELITE SOCIAL MOVEMENT ORGANIZING AND DEFENSE POLICY

Elite Political Organizing

THE PREPONDERANCE OF research examining the political behavior of the greatest wealth holders in the United States indicates
that this group is politically well-organized and probably has a great
deal of influence over the behavior of the state. J. Allen Whitt's (1982,
1979) study of California's mass transit policies during the early
1970s shows that wealthy business elites quickly organize to stop
policies counter to their interests and to promote policies furthering
their interests. Whitt and other researchers have also shown that
business elites are able to build a considerable degree of consensus in
their political endeavors at all levels of political action (Clawson,
Nuestadtl, and Bearden 1986; Mizruchi and Koenig 1986). In fact,
students of the upper class have consistently found that the richest
people and their well-paid professional elites are remarkably well-
organized politically, socially, and economically (Lundberg 1988; Allen 1987; Mintz and Schwartz 1985; Useem 1984, 1983; Domhoff 1983;
1970; Shoup 1980).

A key feature of recent work of this type is that it contends that
significant social and political change results not only from the well-
institutionalized position of the upper class in U.S. society, economy,
and polity or from class conflict, but also from conflicts among factions within the upper class (Ferguson and Rogers 1981; Shoup 1980;

Sale 1976). Jerry Sanders (1983), for example, concludes that intra-class conflicts and the failure of existing upper-class institutions to form a widely inclusive consensus on the path of U.S. foreign policy in the late 1940s, as well as in the 1970s, resulted in significant changes in U.S. foreign policy and subsequent huge increases in military expenditures.

An important aspect of this approach to business-state relations is the emphasis researchers place on organizations, institutions, and material resources as important tools of upper-class domination in contemporary capitalist societies. Existing research indicates that organizations sucy as the Council on Foreign Relations, the Trilateral Commission, the Business Council, The Brookings Institution, and the Atlantic Council are important sources of the power and influence that the upper class has in modern capitalist society (Domhoff 1983; Shoup 1980). Therefore, this study looks to upper-class political organizations for insight into business-state relations. One organization touted as being very influential in recent foreign policy and military policy changes is the Committee on the Present Danger (CPD) (Sanders 1983; Scheer 1982; Shoup 1980). The elite nature of its membership, its apparent influence, and its recent formation make it ideal as a tool to explore the effects of upper-class political action on state policy output. Possibly most important, the CPD is very deeply embedded in the New Right Movement that swept Ronald Reagan to power in the 1980 election.

Most social movement studies, especially those employing resource mobilization theory, tend to omit much discussion of a movement's (movement organization) effect on the state and society (MacDougall 1990).[1] Moreover, there has been important recent work that examines the behavior of contemporary social movements oriented toward making the United States more committed to peace and disarmament, but comparatively little looking at movements seeking a more belligerent and militarized foreign and military policy (for examples, see Klandermans, ed. 1991; Marullo and Lofland, ed. 1990; McCrea and Markle 1989; Holland and Hoover 1985). Consequently, this study adds to the current social movement literature both by examining the effect of a major contemporary social movement on the state and society and by looking at a kind of movement given little space in the contemporary social movement literature.

The primary concern of this chapter is to introduce evidence supporting the idea that wealthy elites in the United States organize into potentially influential social movement organizations to change the general direction of foreign and military policy. I present a case study of the Committee on the Present Danger guided by resource mobilization theory that provides evidence that elites did organize into a social movement organization with the goal of changing the path of military and foreign policy in the United States. This case study forms the basis of a measure of elite political activity I use in my quantitative analysis.

The Committee on the Present Danger

The Committee on the Present Danger was founded in 1976 as a way of countering the campaign promises of newly-elected Jimmy Carter's to reduce military expenditures, to promote self-determination for other nations, to emphasize human rights, and to pursue arms control (Sanders 1983).[2] This organization is deeply embedded in what many scholars call the New Right Movement (Allen 1992; Himmelstein 1990; Hunter 1981; Shoup 1980; Sale 1976). Indeed, I submit that the CPD itself was a core political organ of this movement, the organ focusing New Right political will on changing the military and foreign policy direction of the United States. For example, twenty-four of the founding directors of the CPD are also affiliated with at least one of several new right or neo-conservative think tanks or policy organizations including the Hoover Institute for the Study of War and Revolution, the Georgetown Center for Strategic and International Studies (CSIS), the Heritage Foundation, and the American Enterprise Institute for Public Policy (Sanders 1983; *Who's Who* 1983, 1987; and see Appendix B). Additionally, several of these directors, such as Richard Mellon Scaife, were key leaders in providing funds to support a wide range of New Right political activities (Allen 1992).

An important factor in the committee's creation was Jimmy Carter's total exclusion of all the cold-warrior elites from his administration, despite having two of the most well-respected cold warriors,

Paul Nitze and Dean Rusk, as campaign advisors in 1976 (Shoup 1980; Sanders 1983). Therefore, to remain influential in national politics and promote policies more to their liking, the cold warriors and their wealthy backers had to organize outside the existing mainstream institutional framework built around the Office of the President and elite policy organizations like the Council on Foreign Relations and The Brookings Institution (Shoup 1980; Sanders 1983; Domhoff 1983).

The role of previous elite organizations in the formation of the CPD is quite extensive. The CPD's 141 founding directors came from the ranks of business, the military, labor, academe, and the state. Table 3.1 provides just a sampling of some of the most elite CPD directors and their affiliations. (See Appendix B for a complete list.)

Among the most current prominent members and directors are President Ronald Reagan, David Packard, Nathan Glaser, Saul Bellow, and President George Bush (Committee on the Present Danger 1981). Moreover, the CPD has director interlocks with many very central upper-class policymaking and consensus-building organizations including the Trilateral Commission, the Atlantic Council, the Brookings Institution Board of Trustees, the Business Roundtable, the Business Council, the Committee on Economic Development, and the Council on Foreign Relations. Many directors, such as David Packard, C. Douglas Dillon, and John T. Connor, held positions on several of these policy groups (Shoup 1980; *Who's Who* 1987). Table 3.2 lists the founding directors' past and present affiliations with over seventy policy, political, or philanthropic institutions. These affiliations are as diverse as Nathan Glazer's participation on the Fund for the Republic's Communism in American Life Project during the 1950s to Bayard Rustin's directorship of the A. Philip Randolph Institute (*Who's Who* 1987). The vast majority of CPD directors have been extremely active politically throughout much of their lives.

Not only has the CPD directorship been active in other political organizations, but it has had a great deal of experience with appointed positions in the national government. The directorship includes fifty-one individuals (36 percent of directors) who held key military and civilian government positions before 1976. The important government posts once held by directors were, most commonly,

Table 3.1. A Sampling of Founding Directors of the Committee on the Present Danger and Their Affiliations While the Committee Was Active[a]

Director Name	Affiliation
Theodore C. Achilles	Vice Chairman, Atlantic Council. Former Ambassador, Peru. Director, Eastman Kodak Co., International Management and Development Institute. NATO pact negotiator, Planning conference, CENTO, SEATO, and Columbo organizations. Co-editor, *Atlantic Community Journal* (63–75). Member of the Alibi, Yale, and Brook clubs.
Karl R. Bendetsen[b]	Former Under Secretary of the Army. Consulting Special Assistant to the Secretary of Defense (48). Director General, US. railroads (50–52). Chairman of the Board of Directors, Panama Canal Company. Vice-President of Operations, Champion Paper. CEO, Chairman of the Board, President, Champion International. Director, Member of the Executive Committee, Westinghouse Electric. Governing Board, N.Y. Stock Exchange. Co-head, SDI task force, Heritage Foundation. Directed Evacuation of Japanese from the West Coast. Member of the Links, Metropolitan, Brook, Chicago, Washington Athletic, Bohemian, Pacific Union, Houston Country, Petroleum, Tejas, Bayou, Washington F Street, Georgetown, Everglades, and Bath and Tennis clubs.
John M. Cabot	Former Ambassador to Sudan, Colombia, Brazil, and Poland. Former Assistant Secretary of State for Inter-American Affairs
W. Glenn Campbell	Director, Hoover Institute, Stanford University Advisory Board, Center for Strategic and International Studies, Georgetown. Director, National Science Foundation, Regent, University of California. Member of the Bohemian Grove, Cosmos, and Commonwealth clubs.

Table 3.1. *Continued*

Director Name	Affiliation
Peter B. Clark	President of Evening News Association. Former Chairman, Federal Reserve Bank of Chicago. Member of Detroit Athletic, Detroit Country, and Economics clubs.
John B. Connally	Former Secretary of the Treasury. Former Secretary of the Navy. Former Governor of Texas. Partner, Vinson and Elkins. Director, Justin Industries, Falconbridge Nickel Mines, Ltd.,First City Bancorp of Texas, Inc., First City National Bank of Floresville, Continental Airlines, Inc, and Dr. Pepper Company. Trustee, Andrew W. Mellon Foundation. Member of Houston Chamber of Commerce, Conference Board. Member and Director of the Houston Metropolitan Racquet Club.
John T. Connor	President, Allied Chemical. Former Secretary of Commerce. Director of J. Henry Schroeder Bank and Trust Co., G.M., ABC, Schroders Ltd, and Merck & Company. Member of Business Council, and the Council on Foreign Relations. Trustee Syracuse University.
C. Douglas Dillon	Former Secretary of Treasury. Former Member of US. Stock Exchange. Former Director of US. and Foreign Securities Corp. Director and Chair, Dillon, Reed, & Company. Former Chairman, Rockefeller Foundation. Former Trustee, Brookings Institute. President of Board of Overseers. Harvard University Member of Society of Colonial Wars, New York. Member of the Racquet and Tennis, Knickerbocker, Links, River, Century, Pilgrims, and Metropolitan clubs.

Table 3.1. *Continued*

Director Name	Affiliation
Henry H. Fowler	Partner, Goldman, Sachs & Co. Former Secretary of the Treasury. Vice Chairman Atlantic Council. Member of the Conference Board. Member of the Recess River (NYC), Links, and Metropolitan clubs.
William H. Franklin	Former Chairman, Caterpillar Tractor Co.
Peter H. B. Frelinghuysen	Former Congressman Investment Broker (NYC). Trustee, Howard Savings Bank.
J. Peter Grace	President, W.R. Grace & Company. Director, Brascom Ltd, Ingorsoll-Rand Co., Stove and Webster, Inc., Omnicare, Roto Rooter Inc., Universal Furniture Ltd. and Miliken & Company. Trustee, Atlantic Mutual,Incorporated. Director, Boys Club of America. Chairman, Radio Free Europe. Trustee, Grace Institute. Member of Council on Foreign Relations. Member of Racquet and Tennis, Madison Square Garden, Links, India House, Meadow Brook, Pacific Union, and Everglades clubs.
J.C. Hurewitz	Director, The Middle East Institute, Columbia University. Former researcher, Rand Corporation. Consultant to the Departments of State and Defense. Council on Foreign Relations, ABC News, Stanford Research Institute, and International Institute for Strategic Studies.
Belton K. Johnson	Chairman, Chaporrosa Agri-Services Incorporated. Former Manager, King Ranch, TX. Director, Campbell Soup, ST&T, Tenneco, First City Bancorp of TX. Former Director of Active Communication on Critical Choices for Americans. Former Co-Chair, Republican National Committee. Member of the Capital Hill, River, Racquet and Tennis, Cover Valley, Rod and Gun, Order of the Alamo, and Links clubs.

Table 3.1. *Continued*

Director Name	Affiliation
Max M. Kampelman	Attorney, Fried, Frank, Harris, Shriver & Kampelman. Chairman and Former Director, District of Columbia National Bank. Director, Georgetown University. Director, Atlantic Council. Member of the Cosmos, Federal City, and National Press clubs.
Leon H. Keyserling	President and Founder, Conference on Economic Progress. Chairman, Council of Economic Advisors under President Truman. Director of"various companies." Member of the Cosmos, Harvard, and Columbia University (Washington, D.C.) clubs.
James A. Linen IV	Director and former President of Time Incorporated. Executive Vice-President, National Enquirer (1976–7). Owner, Des Plaines Publishers. Vice-President, Media General Incorporated. CEO, Media General Broadcast Services, Incorporated. Chairman of the Board, American Thai Corporation. Member, Economic, Racquet of Chicago, Round Hill, Country of Virginia, Commonwealth, Yale, Brook, and Farmington Country clubs.
Clare Boothe Luce	Author, Former Member of Congress. Ambassador to Italy. Member, Academy of Policy Science, American Institute for Foreign Trade. Director, American Security. Council Member, Hawaii's Foundation of American Freedom, US. Strategic Institute, and the Daughters of the American Revolution.

Table 3.1. *Continued*

Director Name	Affiliation
Donald S. MacNaughton	Chairman and CEO, The Prudential Insurance Company. CEO, Hospital Corporation. Chair, Executive Committee, Exxon Corporation. Director, Third National Corp., New York Stock Exchange, Trustee Vanderbilt University. Member, Business Council. Member of the Eastward Ho, Sailfish Point, Links, and Belle Meade clubs.
William McChesney Martin, Jr.	Former Chairman, Federal Reserve Board. Member New York Stock Exchange (31–38). Board of Directors, Import-Export Bank. Chair, Federal Reserve Board (51–70). Director, Freeport Minerals Co. and Scandinavian Securities Corporation. Member of the West Side Tennis, Yale, Metropolitan, Alibi, and Chevy Chase clubs.
George C. McGhee	Former Under Secretary of State for Public Affairs. Former Ambassador to Turkey. Owner McGhee Production Co. (oil). Chairman of the Board, *Saturday Review.* Director, Mobil Corp., Procter & Gamble Co., American Security Bank, and Transworld Airlines. Member, Atlantic Council. Director, Vasser College and American University. Member of the Metropolitan, City Tavern, Brook, and Bohemenian Grove clubs.
Thomas S. Nichols	President, Nichols Company. Former Chairman, Executive Committee, Olin Corporation.

Table 3.1. *Continued*

Director Name	Affiliation
George Olmsted	Chairman and CEO, International Bank, Washington, D.C. Chairman, First Insurance and Finance Co., United Security Insurance Company. Director, Northeastern Insurance Co., Hawkeye Insurance Co., United Security Insurance Co., International Bank, International General Industries Inc., General Service Life Co., and Bankers Security Life Company. Founder, United Federal Savings and Loan Association. Chairman, I.B. Credit Corporation, Avis Industrial Corp, Woodman Co., Woodman Co, and Kliklok Corp., New York City. Member of the Shriners, Metropolitan, Army-Navy and Washington Golf and Country clubs.
David Packard	Chairman of the Board, Hewlett-Packard Company. Former Deputy Secretary of Defense. Director, Gentech and Boeing Company. Member, Trilateral Commission, Atlantic Council, American Enterprise Institute for Public Policy, Board of Overseers, Hoover Institute, Business Roundtable, Trustee, Herbert Hoover Foundation and Stanford University. Member of the Bohemian Grove, Commonwealth, Pacific Union, Worldtrade, Links, Alfalfa, Capital Hill, and California clubs.
H. Chapman Rose	Former Under Secretary of the Treasury. Board of Directors, Atlantic Council. Trustee Emeritus, Princeton University and Brookings Institute. Member of the Union, Tavern, Kirkland Country, Princeton, Metropolitan, Burning Tree and Chevy Chase clubs.

Table 3.1. *Continued*

Director Name	Affiliation
Charles E. Saltzman	Partner, Goldman, Sachs & Company. Former Under Secretary of State for Administration. Partner, Henry Sears and Co. (49–56). Member, English Speaking Union of the US. (pres. 61–66). Member of the University, Union, Downtown Association, Century Association, and Pilgrim clubs.
<u>Richard Mellon Scaife</u>	Publisher, <u>Tribune-Review</u>. Director, Sarah Scaife Foundation. President, Paraffin Oil Corporation.
Lloyd H. Smith	President Paraffin Oil Corporation. Vice President, Argus Research Corp. Executive Director, City National Bank Houston. Director, National Review, Curtiss-Wright Corp., Info Storage Systems, Falcon Seaboard Inc. Trustee Pine Mountain College. Member of the Bayou, Ramada, Tejas, Everglades, Racquet and Tennis, Brook, River, National Golf, Links, Southampton, and Meadow Clubs.
Arthur Temple	Chairman of the Board, President and C.E.O., Temple-Eastex Inc.
Charles E. Walker	Charles E. Walker Associates, Incorporated. Former Deputy Secretary of the Treasury. Vice-President, Republic National Bank Dallas. Executive Vice-President, Bankers Association, NYC. Director, Enron Corp., Potomac Electric Power Co., Tracor Inc., and USF & G Corporation. Chairman, American Council for Capital Formation. Co-Chairman, Bretton Woods Committee. Member, Council on Foreign Relations. Member of the Union League, Burning Tree, and Congressional clubs.

[a]Adapted from Shoup (1980) and Sanders (1983), Affiliations from Who's Who in America (1982, 1988)
[b]Individuals with direct affiliations with New Right foundations and thinktanks described by Himmelstein (1990) and Allen (1989) are shown underlined.

Table 3.2. Organizations with Ties to the Founding Board of Directors of the
Committee on the Present Danger

Organization	Number of Ties
Thinktanks	
Foreign Policy Research Institute	1
Academy for Policy Science	1
American Enterprise Institute	3
American Institute for Foreign Trade	1
Brookings Institute	4
Center for Strategic and International Studies	7
Hoover Institute	7
Hudson Institute	3
International Center for Economic and Policy Analysis	1
International Institute for Strategic Studies	8
Business Consensus Building and Policy Groups	
Atlantic Council	10
Atlantic Union	2
Business Council	2
Business Roundtable	1
Committee for Economic Development	1
Conference Board	2
Council on Foreign Relations	16
National Planning Association	4
Trilateral Commission	3
Political and Lobbying Organizations	
American Security Council	1
Americans for Energy Independence	2
Coalition for a Democratic Majority	2
Association to Unite the Democracies	1
Committee for a Free World	2
Commission on Critical Choices	1
Democratic National Committee	2
Committee to Re-elect the President (Nixon)	1
Republican National Committee	1
US. Strategic Institute	2
National Strategic Information Center	1
Social Democrats USA	1
Minneapolis Committee for a Secure Middle East	1
Americans for Democratic Action	1
Foundations and Philanthropic Organizations	
Sarah Scaife Foundation	1
B'nai Brith Hillel Foundation	1

Table 3.2. *Continued*

Organization	Number of Ties
United Way	1
Rockefeller Foundation	2
George C. Marshall Foundation	1
Herbert Hoover Foundation	1
Andrew Mellon Fund	1
Professional and Other Groups	
A. Philip Randalph Institute	2
American Association for the Advancement of Science	1
Center for the Study of Liberty in America	1
Citizen's Committee for International Development	1
Civil Liberties Union of Massachusetts	1
Colonial Society of Massachusetts	1
Communism in American Life Project	1
Conference on Economic Progress	1
Fund for the Republic	1
National Association for the Advancement of Colored People	1
National Academy of Science	1
National Urban League	1
National Counsel on the Humanities	1
National Science Foundation	1
Public Broadcasting Stations	1
Smithsonian Institution	1
Society of Colonial Wars (NYC)	1

in the Department of the Treasury (8), in civilian military administration (6), as ambassadors (6), and as uniformed officers (5).

In keeping with the tradition of other upper-class organizations, the CPD also has several representatives from organized labor (Burris 1992; Domhoff 1983). Lane Kirkland of the AFL-CIO is a director of the CPD and the Council on Foreign Relations. The American Federation of Teachers and the International Ladies Garment Workers' Union both have two representatives on the CPD's board of directors. The Amalgamated Clothing and Textile Workers Union, Ironworkers International Union, International Union of Operating Engineers, and the Plumbers and Pipe Fitters International Union all have at least one representative, usually a high official, holding a CPD directorship (Sanders 1983).

The largest single group of current occupations listed for directors of the CPD is university professor or president. Forty of the forty-eight directors with academic backgrounds are, or were, university faculty. The other eight directors are, or were, university presidents. The universities contributing directors to the CPD include Yale Law School, Sarah Lawrence College, Howard University, Georgetown University (home of the very conservative and politically active Center for Strategic and International Studies), the University of Wisconsin, Harvard University, Fletcher School of Law and Diplomacy, and many other prestigious institutions (Sanders 1983; Shoup 1980). This list of faculty includes such well-known and respected individuals as Seymour Martin Lipset of Stanford University, Nathan Glaser of Harvard University, and Edward Teller, father of the hydrogen bomb and very influential supporter of the strategic defense initiative. With the exceptions of Howard University, Lake Erie College and the University of South Carolina, all twenty-three universities and colleges with academic connections to the CPD were among the top 100 universities receiving Department of Defense contracts in the late 1960s (Pursell 1972). Thus, the academic contingent of the founding directors of the CPD was not from the fringes of the university community as were some prominent New Right academics, but rather from the very core of the mainstream academic community.

The CPD reflects a classic pattern of upper-class political groups as described by G. W. Domhoff and other scholars of the upper class (Domhoff 1983; Shoup 1980; Useem 1983). The CPD's founding directors included members of the upper class, managers of major corporations, leaders of a few major labor unions, and members of prestigious academic institutions. The upper class and their helpers, the power elite, are well-represented on the CPD.

The CPD is, with little doubt, an upper-class political organization. For example, Table 3.3 lists the eighty-two elite private clubs in which the founding directors held memberships during the early 1980s. About 18 percent of these clubs (15) are listed by G. W. Domhoff (1983) as being among the most elite and prestigious of national and regional upper-class social clubs in the United States. Additionally, many of the founders have been directors, chief execu-

Table 3.3. Club Membership of Committee of the Present Danger's Founding
Board of Directors

Organization Name	Number of Members on the CPD
Alfalfa	1
Alibi	2
Army-Navy	1
Bath and Tennis	1
Bayou	2
Belle Meadow	1
Boar's Head	1
Bohemian*	4
Broad Street	1
Brook*	4
Burning Tree	3
California Clubs*	1
Capital Hill	3
Center	1
Century*	3
Chevy Chase	2
Chicago*	1
City Tavern	2
Clover Valley	1
Colonnade	1
Columbia University	1
Commonwealth	3
Cosmos	13
Country of Virginia	1
Daughters of the American Revolution*	1
Detroit Athletic*	1
Detroit Country	1
Downtown Association	1
Eastward Ho	1
Economics	2
Elizabethan	1
Everglades*	3
Farmington Country	1
Federal City	2
Georgetown	1
Harvard	3
Houston Metropolitan Racquet Club	1
India House	1

Table 3.3. *Continued*

Organization Name	Number of Members on the CPD
International	3
Kenwood	2
Kirkland Country	1
Knickerbocker*	1
Links*	1
Masons	1
Meadow	1
Meadow Brook	1
Metropolitan	9
National Press Clubs	2
New Haven Lawn*	3
Order of the Alamo	1
Oxford Union	1
Pacific Union*	3
Petroleum	1
Pilgrims	2
Princeton	2
Racquet and Tennis	4
Racquet of Chicago	1
Recess River*	1
River*	3
Rod and Gun	1
Round Hill	1
Sailfish Point	1
Shriners	2
Tejas	2
Union*	5
University Club	1
Washington Athletic	1
Washington F Street	1
Washington Golf and Country	1
West Side Tennis	1
Worldtrade	1
Yale	4

*Club is listed in G. W. Domhoff's Who Rules America Now as an Upper Class social club or organization.

tive officers, presidents, vice presidents, or owners of 110 businesses, forty-three of them insurance, banking, or investment firms, and thirty-four of them industrial or primary extraction firms (see Table 3.4 for the complete list and Table 3.5 for the breakdown by type of firm). Among the founding directors' affiliations are some of the largest and most influential companies in the United States, including Citibank, Time Inc.; Prudential Insurance Co. of America; Olin Corporation; Caterpillar Tractor; Stroock, Stroock, and Lavan; and Dillon, Reed, and Co. (*Who's Who* 1987; Sanders 1983).

Among the CPD's 141 directors and executive committee members are forty-two individuals whose multiple directorships, memberships in elite social clubs such as the Bohemian Grove, and other corporate leadership positions would classify them, according to Domhoff (1983, 1974), as members of the national upper class. Indeed, the directorship ties, participation in policymaking groups, government positions, and social club memberships would place the majority of these people in the category Useem (1984) calls the inner circle; these are the central movers and shakers of this nation's economy and polity. This list includes David Packard, part owner of Hewlett-Packard, Richard Mellon Scaife, Arthur Temple, Mary Pillsbury Lord, C. Douglas Dillon, John M. Cabot, John T. Connor, and J. Peter Grace (Lundberg 1988; Allen 1987; *Who's Who* 1987; Sanders 1983; Shoup 1980).

Another important facet of the CPD is the source of CPD funds. For many reasons, not the least of which is the desire for anonymity by many benefactors of the CPD, discovery of information on where the CPD gets its money is much more difficult than researching its directorships. Jerry Sanders (1983) notes that a major benefactor of the CPD and of other conservative organizations who has worked very closely with the CPD is Richard Mellon Scaife. Scaife gave $260,000 to the CPD between 1977 and 1981. The Sarah Scaife Foundation, chaired by Richard Mellon Scaife, gave the Heritage Foundation $3.8 million, the Hoover Institution $3.5 million, the National Strategy Information Center $6 million, and the Center for Strategic and International Studies at Georgetown University $5.3 million during the late 1970s and early 1980s (Sanders 1983). The CSIS, an institutional base for many of the CPD academic and ex-government directors, also received significant donations from the J. Howard

Table 3.4. Corporations with Ties to the Committee on the Present Danger's
Founding Board of Directors

ABC	First Insurance Company
Allied Chemical	First National Bank of Floresville
American Building Maintenance	First National Bank of Minneapolis
Industries	Frank, Harris, Shriver, and
American Medical Building Inc.	Kampelman
American Security Bank	Freeport Mineral Company
American Thai Corporation	Gateway National Bank of St. Louis
Argus Research	General Motors
Atlantic Mutual Inc.	General Security Life Company
Avis Industrial Corporation	Gentech
Avis International Corporation	Georgia-Pacific
Barker Security Life Company	Gifford Hill and Company
Beneficial Corporation	Globe Security Systems
Boeing	Goldman, Sachs and Company
Bullock Funds	Hawkeye Insurance Company
Caterpillar Tractor Company	Henry Schroeder Bank and Trust
Champion International	Company
Chaporrosa Agri-Services, Inc.	Hewlett-Packard Inc.
Charles E. Walker and Associates	Honeywell
Citibank Inc.	Hospital Corporation of America
Cohn and Marks	Howard Savings Bank
Concept Associates	I.B. Credit Corporation
Continental Airlines	Information Storage Systems Inc.
Crane and Rusack Inc.	Ingersoll Rand
Curtiss-Wright	International Bank of Washington,
Des Plaines Publishing	D.C.
Digital Recording Corporation	International General Industries Inc.
Dillon, Reed, and Company	Justin Industries
District of Columbia National Bank	Kliklok Corporation of NYC
Dr. Pepper	Media General Inc.
Drilling and Products Company	Merck and Company
Eastman Kodak	Miliken and Company
Enron Corporation	Millipore Corporation
Esmark Inc.	Mobil Oil
Exxon Corporation	National Bank of Houston
Falcon Seaboard Inc.	National Enquirer
Falconbridge Nickel Mines	National Review
Federal Reserve Bank of Chicago	National Savings and Trust Company
First America Bank (Wa. DC)	Neville Associates
First City Bancorp of Texas	New York Life Insurance Company

Table 3.4. *Continued*

New York Stock Exchange	Stroock, Stroock and Lavin
Nichols Company	Student Loan Marketing Association
Northeastern Insurance Company	Temple-Eastex Inc.
Olin Corporation	Third National Bank
Omnicare	Time Inc.
Paraffin Oil	Transway International
Phelps-Stokes Fund	Transworld Airlines
Potomac International Incorporated	US. and Foreign Securities
Proctor and Gamble	Corporation
Prudential Insurance Company of	Unicorp America
America	United Savings and Loan Association
Readers Digest Inc.	United Security Insurance Company
Republic National Bank of Dallas	Universal Finance Ltd.
RMI Corporation	USA Funds Inc.
Roto-Rooter Inc.	USF&G Corporation
Safeway Corporation	Vinson and Ellies
Scandinavian Securities Corporation	Wickes Company Inc.
Schroeder Ltd.	Woodman Company
Stone and Webster Inc.	Zumwalt and Associates

Pew foundation, the John M. Olin Foundation (represented on the CPD by Thomas S. Nichols), the S. R. Noble Foundation, and the H. Smith Richelson Foundation (Muscative 1986). Various researchers have linked all of these organizations to the New Right Movement (Allen 1992; Himmelstein 1990; Shoup 1983)

Table 3.5. Distribution of Firms with Ties to the Founding Board of Directors of the Committee on the Present Danger by Type

Firm Type	Number	Percent
Financial	43	39%
Big Industrials	34	33
Media	7	6
Transportation	2	2
Other*	21	19
Total	110	100%

*Includes firms of unknown type, plus consulting, small firms, import/ export, retail, and services.

It is noteworthy that in its 1976 statement of goals and guidelines the CPD wrote:

> We are limiting annual contributions from a single source to $10,000. Our objective is a broad base of public support. For special projects, particularly those appropriate for foundation support and not contained in our regular budget, we may accept larger amounts.
> Under no circumstances, will we solicit or accept contributions from companies or persons who derive a substantial portion of their income from the defense industry.
> "How the Committee on the Present Danger will Operate—What It Will Do, and What It Will Not Do" 11 November 1976

These guidelines do not rule out directors connected to the defense industry, nor do they rule out donations from foundations linked to defense industrialists.

The resources the directors of the CPD could potentially use to further the CPD's goal of remilitarizing the United States' relationship with the rest of the world are astounding. The resources linked to the Olin family, for example, include a $50 million foundation, a $300 million family fortune, and a significant, if not controlling, interest in the $1.6 billion Olin Corporation (Allen 1987; *Standard and Poor's* 1979). Richard Mellon Scaife is the director of the $200 million Sarah Scaife Foundation and has family ties to the Mellon fortune which was worth at least $6 billion in 1984. Allen (1987) reports that David Packard and his family were worth at least $2.1 billion in 1986. John M. Cabot is a member of the highly visible Cabot family, worth over $350 million in 1979. This family is noted for having many distinguished businessmen, diplomats, and influential professionals among its members (Lundberg 1988; Burch 1980).[3]

Along with the personal and family fortunes connected to CPD members and directors, the CPD could also tap considerable institutional and organizational resources to further its goals. CPD membership includes the leaders and members of eleven large and powerful labor unions, such as the United Auto Workers; twenty-three prestigious universities; and many Fortune 500 firms, including Exxon Corp., Mobil Oil Corp., General Motors, and Allied Chemical. Finally, there are CPD members with ties to banks such as

Citibank with over $74 billion worth of deposits in 1979 (the largest bank in the United States and the ninth largest in the world based on total deposits), as well as insurance firms such as Prudential Insurance Company of American, the largest insurance firm in the United States. Add to these resources the political, public relations, organizational, and ideological experiences of the directorship and the potential resource base of the CPD, even if only a tiny part of the available economic resources were available, is incomparable to most any well-known social movement organization operating in the last thirty years.

While the CPD certainly has not been able to mobilize all the resources linked to its directorship and members, it has undertaken many activities to further its cause. It goes beyond the purview of this book to describe all the political actions of the CPD, but the CPD annual report for 1979 does give a sampling of some of the work done by the CPD. During 1979,

1. Members testified seventeen times before Congress, more than all other critics together;
2. Paul Nitze's SALT II paper was updated eleven times;
3. 479 television and radio programs, press conferences, debates, public forums, etc., were given for citizen leaders; and
4. 400,000 copies of pamphlets and reports were distributed (Sanders, 269).

The CPD and its members also provided ideological guidance to more than fifty affiliated pro-military political groups by publishing and authoring numerous policy papers, reports and studies. The CPD became the umbrella organization for many groups trying to increase military spending and restart the cold war. From 1978 through 1980, the SALT II treaty was the focus of much of the CPD's and its affiliated organizations' political efforts. Before the Carter administration had completed the treaty negotiations, the CPD had spent over $750,000 to stop the ratification of this treaty (*Christian Science Monitor* 1979). Affiliated organizations spending larger amounts of money to stop SALT II included the Coalition for Peace Through Strength with $2.5 million, the American Security Council with $3 million, and the Conservative Caucus with $1 million. Opponents of SALT II spent about fourteen times as much money as did treaty supporters (*Christian Science Monitor* 1979). Another hot issue of the time was the Panama Canal Treaty, targeted for $1.8 million in effort by the American Conservative Union (Sanders 1983).

Directors of the CPD also proved to be influential in the academic policy debates surrounding U.S. strategic and military policy. Richard Pipes's article in *Commentary*,[4] entitled "Why the Soviet Union Thinks it Could Fight and Win a Nuclear War" (1977), was the first in a long series of widely cited and influential anti-Soviet articles to come from directors and members of the CPD. Colin S. Gray, though not a director of the CPD, had collegial relationships with several of its directors and had affiliations with several of their home institutions, including Richard Pipes and the Hudson Institute. Gray did a great deal to further the CPD's cause with his variously titled pieces on political decapitation strategies and victory in nuclear war (see Gray 1981). Some other influential and prolific CPD members and associates responsible for developing and disseminating the neo-cold warrior ideology of the CPD include Edward N. Luttwak (1978), Daniel O. Graham (1977), Paul Nitze (1976–77), and Donald G. Brennan (1975).

A common thread running through the intellectual work of the CPD and affiliated academics is a very questionable presentation of the military and political relationship between the Soviet Union and the United States. For example, Colin S. Gray (1978) presents data on expected capabilities of Soviet inter-continental ballistic missiles (ICBMs) for the 1980s. Gray estimated the warhead yield for the SS-18 (the most formidable of Soviet ICBMs) as over 2 megatons (over 117 times the yield of the bomb dropped on Hiroshima). Government organizations in the late 1970s put the upper bounds for this warhead at about 1.5 megatons, high confidence estimates at 1 megaton, and the most common estimate at .550 megaton (Aldridge 1978). By the early 1980s the Reagan administration firmly put the SS-18 warhead yield at .55 megatons (Dennis 1984).

Equally biased estimates (based on little or no accurate information) for warhead accuracy, silo hardness, and number of warheads per booster were present throughout CPD documents and articles by affiliated academics. Because these numbers are very important components of computer simulations predicting the outcomes of nuclear weapons exchanges,[5] by using these biased estimates the cold warriors could seem to provide empirical evidence supporting their positions of United States vulnerability to Soviet attack and of the Soviet intention to use nuclear blackmail against the United States. Because the data on many of the performance characteristics of most of the United States' and Soviet Union's nuclear weapons are unavailable to most scholars, and because much of the classified information is difficult to interpret or unreliable, the CPD did not fear criticisms based on well-documented data (Tsipsis 1982). Moreover, because the major sources of much of this type of data, the U.S. military and the Central Intelligence Agency (CIA), shared many of the same policy goals of the CPD there was very little chance that government organizations would expose the work of the CPD as social movement ideology cloaked in the trappings of mainstream scholarship.

One of the principal targets of these tactics was public opinion, both the attitudes of opinion leaders, such as government and business officials, and the general public. For example, in 1976 several founding directors were managers or owners of media companies including the Evening News Association, Time, Inc., Readers Digest Co., *Policy Review,* Des Plaines Publishers, and *The Tribune-Review.* Directors were editors or major contributors to thirteen journals, dailies, and news magazines, including *The National Review, Commentary, The Saturday Review,* and *Orbis.* Table 3.6 provides a complete list of media firms connected to the CPD's founding board of directors. In a mobilization against other elites, the general public is a functionally neutral party, but public opinion does affect governmental decisions.[6] Thus, by motivating the general public to support their policies, the CPD could gain leverage over the competing elite factions. One of the principal purposes of creating the CPD was to provide the pro-military elites an independent source for disseminating information (Sanders 1983).

Sanders elegantly states the goals of this elite group: "From its founding on the heels of Carter's 1976 victory, the CPD's goal has been unequivocal: to resurrect a militarized doctrine of containment

Table 3.6. Editorships and Management Positions with Print Media Held by Founding Board Members of the Committee on the Present Danger

Firm	Number of CPD Held Positions
Asian Affairs	1
Atlantic Community Journal	1
Commentary	2
Daedulus	1
Des Plaines Publisher	1
Evening News Association	1
Fortune Magazine	1
Global Affairs	1
International Security Review	1
National Enquirer	1
National Review	2
Orbis	1
Policy Review	1
Readers Digest	1
Saturday Review	1
Strategic Review	1
Time Incorporated	1
Tribune Review	1
Wall Street Journal	1

as the cornerstone of United States foreign policy" (1983, 8). Indeed, it appears the CPD was very successful in achieving its objectives. Sanders stated further,

> By 1980 Carter's original stated goal of nuclear disarmament, pledge of non-intervention, and promised rollback in military spending were no more. In their place military spending was on the rise, intervention was once more sanctioned with the announcement of the Carter Doctrine, etc., etc. Privately the CPD must have rejoiced at the turn of events (270).

The efficacy of the CPD's efforts dramatically increased when Ronald Reagan took office in 1981. The President appointed many of the directors and members of the CPD to central positions in the White House foreign policy and national security elite. Table 3.7 lists the thirty-three directors and members of the CPD, including Reagan, who had taken key positions in the White House or other gov-

Table 3.7. CPD Appointees to President Reagan's Administration as of 1985[a]

Director Name	Administrative Post
Kenneth L. Adelman	U.S. Deputy Representative to the UN
Richard V. Allen	Assistant to the President for National Security Affairs
Martin Anderson	Assistant to the President for Policy Development
James L. Buckley	Under Secretary of State for Security Assistance, Science and Technology
W. Glenn Campbell[b]	Chairman, The Intelligence Oversight Board Member, President's Foreign Intelligence Advisory Board
William J. Casey	Director, CIA
John B. Connally	Member, President's Foreign Intelligence Advisory Board
Joseph D. Douglass, Jr.	Assistance Director, ACDA
John S. Foster, Jr.	Member, President's Foreign Intelligence Advisory Board
Amoretta M. Hoeber	Deputy Assistant Secretary of the Army for Research and Development
Fred Charles Ikle	Under Secretary of Defense for Policy
Max M. Kampelman	Chairman, U.S. Delegation to Conference on Security and Cooperation in Europe
Geoffrey Kemp	Staff, National Security Council
Jeane J. Kirkpatrick	U.S. Representative to the UN
John F. Lehman	Secretary of the Navy
Clare Boothe Luce	Member, President's Foreign Intelligence Advisory Board
Paul H. Nitze	Chief Negotiator for Theater Nuclear Forces
Edward E. Noble	Chairman, U.S. Synthetic Fuels Corporation
Michael Novak	U.S. Representative on the Human Rights Commission of the Economic and Social Council of the UN
Peter O'Donnell, Jr.	Member President's Foreign Intelligence Advisory Board
Richard N. Perle	Assistant Secretary of Defense for International Security Policy
Richard Pipes	Staff, National Security Council
Eugene V. Rostow	Director, ACDA
Paul Seabury	Member, President's Foreign Intelligence Advisory Board
George P. Shultz	Chairman, President's Economic Policy Advisory Board

Table 3.7. *Continued*

Director Name	Administrative Post
R. G. Stilwell	Deputy Under Secretary of Defense for Policy
Robert Strausz-Hupe	Ambassador to Turkey
Charles Tyroler, II	Member The Intelligence Oversight Board
William R. Van Cleave	Chairman-Designate, General Advisory Committee, ACDA
Charles E. Walker	Member President's Economic Policy Advisory Board
Seymour Weiss	member, President's Foreign Intelligence Advisory Board
Edward Bennett Williams	Member, President's Foreign Intelligence Advisory Board

aAdapted from Then Committee on the Present Danger (1985).
bIndividuals with direct affiliations with New Right foundations and thinktanks described by Himmelstein (1990) and Allen (1989, 1987) are underlined.

ernment posts by 1985 (CPD 1985). The CPD supplied sixty people to the government and to influential advisory bodies. (Tyroler 1984)

Among the key positions taken by CPD members and directors included Secretary of the Navy John F. Lehman, Chief Negotiator for Theater Nuclear Forces Paul Nitze, Secretary of State George P. Schultz, United States Representative to the United Nations Jeanne J. Kirkpatrick, and Director of the CIA William Casey.

Robert Scheer of the *Los Angeles Times* wrote, "The personnel and perspectives of the Committee are represented amply on the Reagan foreign policy team. Reagan himself belonged to the 150 [*sic*] member committee, and twenty-three other members now hold top positions in his administration. The list read like a partial *Who's Who* of the Reagan Administration" (*Los Angeles Times*, August 28, 1981 quoted in CPD 1985, 11). The outsiders of the 1970s had become the insiders of the 1980s.

Many authors, scholars, and organizations, including the John Birch Society, well-known journalists such as Robert Scheer, and scholars such as Laurence Shoup and Jerry W. Sanders, have suggested the CPD had great influence over the United States' foreign and military policies. Although probably overstated, among the successes claimed by the CPD, its promoters, and its detractors are:

1. replacing the Carter "appeasement oriented" (in the words of the CPD) foreign policy elite with old and young cold warriors;
2. profoundly changing public opinion toward favoring more military spending and a more belligerent and bellicose foreign policy (although the best documented polls showed changes in public opinion lasting only a few years);
3. stopping the ratification of SALT II;
4. boosting military spending;
5. stopping detente;
6. putting Ronald Reagan into office; and
7. giving respectability to what were once considered alarmist and extremist views.

Once the Reagan administration had hired many of the most active and important directors and members of the CPD, it became less visible and certainly less politically active. For many key figures, such as Eugene Rostow of Yale Law School, Richard Pipes of Harvard University, and Paul Nitze of Johns Hopkins University, as well as others both inside and outside academe, the movement from jobs allowing them to pursue CPD political activities to jobs with high administrative and travel workloads must have severely curtailed their social movement activities. Additionally, once inside the institutions originally targeted by the social movement, they could no longer lobby as challenging groups; instead, the CPD leadership now found itself in the unenviable position of being a target for other social movement organizations! The co-optation or institutionalization of social movement organizations is a common path to their ultimate dissolution (McCrea and Markle 1989; Piven and Cloward 1977). Despite this potential, the most common ambition of a social movement organization is to have its goals legitimized by the state. Indeed, inclusion of the group into the cadre of state managers is the highest level of "acceptance" a social movement organization can attain (Gamson 1975).

The CPD, according to Sanders and many other authors, proved to be a very influential organization. By about 1983, however, after having many of its members take high level positions in the White House, including the President of the United States, the organization began to wind down its activities, largely content with the direction of United States foreign and military policy. The CPD is still formally operating today, but with many of its key activists either in government or taking up other interests such as making money. It is no longer as active and influential as it was during the last two years of the Carter administration and the first years of the Reagan administration.

Another potential causative force in the decline of the CPD was the apparent withdrawal of key sources of support. McCrea and Markle's (1989) study of the nuclear freeze movement cites data from the Forum Institute (1985) detailing the upsurge of foundation support for groups and organizations furthering liberal and traditional mainstream approaches to international conflict, for example, traditional deterrence theory, conflict management, and arms control. The Forum Institute documents an increase of more than 200 percent in this type of support from less than $16 million in 1982 to over $52 million in 1984. Among the foundation contributors cited by the Forum Institute as supporters of the liberal establishment orientation are organizations such as the J. Howard Pew foundation, which was once a top supporter of groups such as the CPD. Possibly this increasing support for "liberal establishment" perspectives on the arms race by major upper-class institutions represented either a shift in upper-class support away from the new cold warrior perspective of the CPD to the more mainstream deterrence orientation. On the other hand, it perhaps could be the result of the mobilizing of the liberal faction of capital into a social movement of its own to counter the successes of the CPD and the rest of the New Right.

Whatever the source of the reduction in the apparent effect of the CPD on U.S. military and foreign policies, the high-profile contributions of the CPD to the political direction of the national government present in the late 1970s and early 1980s largely ceased by 1985. The CPD has ceased distributing new publications, updating older publications, and sending fundraising letters (I used to get two or more per year, this tapered off to an occasional letter by the mid-1980s, and by the end of the 1980s the letters stopped entirely). I visited the CPD office in Washington, D.C. during the summer of 1986 where I found a sleepy, but tastefully decorated, office facility inhabited by a secretary, a couple of young interns, and an administrative assistant.

The Committee on the Present Danger is an important organization in a number of ways. It is an organization tied very closely to organizations and individuals that are central to the recent New Right political movement. The CPD is a social movement organization made up almost exclusively of elites from the central government, the military, and the highest reaches of the business community.[7] The committee, through a wide range of tactics, appears to have been a remarkably successful social movement organization, gaining not only recognition, but actual participation, in the governing process. The fact that members of the CPD were able to move from being outside the state to positions at the top of the hierarchy of state managers makes it clear that when studied over time, the common dichotomy made between state managers and the rest of society by some recent theories of the state is inappropriate. The activities of the CPD indicate that politically organized members of society attempt to influence the state both from outside the state and from positions in the state. How much influence the CPD or its larger parent, the New Right social movement, has had on U.S. military policy, however, remains unclear.

Measurement of New Right Social Movement Activity

A key question remains: did the CPD influence policy during its period of activity? Many journalists and some scholars suggest this is so, but no numerical assessment of its effects have yet been made. A simple dichotomous variable, coded 1 for when the committee was organized and 0 otherwise, first appeared to be an easy and appropriate way of testing the effects of the CPD activity on my procurement data series. However, the activity of the Committee on the Present Danger has varied from year to year. For much of my series of procurement data the CPD was not organized and during its first year of existence it did little political action. By 1977, however, the level of publicly documented activity began to increase substantially and by 1979, during the SALT II hearings, the activity of the committee began to reach its highest levels. In 1984, after several years of high activity and great successes, the activity of the committee slackened and by 1987, though it still sent out press releases and published an occasional pamphlet assessing the policies of the Reagan administration, the CPD was essentially in a state of political hibernation.[8] Although examining the causes of these changes in behavior go beyond the scope of this book, the fact of these changes calls for a measure of CPD activity that acknowledges these fluctuations in committee activity.

Because I did not have sufficient resources to assess the activity of the CPD with dollars spent or press releases produced, I use a more subjective measure of CPD activity. Moreover, because the CPD's political activity has been multidimensional, with much undocumented activity taking place, no accurate objective measure of CPD behavior is likely to be possible. Consequently, I use a measure of CPD behavior derived from the work of Sanders (1983), articles in *The New York Times*, and in academic journals by directors of the CPD, and the number of CPD members remaining in White House positions. I measure CPD activity with a variable coded 0 for the year the CPD was either not organized or largely inactive (as it has been since 1984), 1 for when the committee was operating at its peak level of activity, and .25 and .50 for years when the CPD was at intermediate levels of activity. I derived these codes by examining the academic and popular literature, especially *The New York Times* and *The Washington Post Weekly*, for articles and books written by committee directors or members, and by looking to Sanders's (1983) discussions of CPD activity for insight into changes in activity over time. This subjective composite of these sources provides a good measure of the relative level of CPD political activity from year to year without the potentially misleading accuracy of a more systematic counting of a single dimension of CPD action. Keep in mind, however, that the measure I use in this analysis is, at best, a crude measure of the actual behavior of the CPD and is likely to have missed some important aspects of CPD political behavior.

Most of the CPD's activity was directed toward developing a more belligerent foreign and military policy stance toward the Soviet Union, increasing U.S. covert and overt intervention in the affairs of other nations,[9] and increasing military readiness in all areas (Sanders

1983). CPD ideology gave special emphasis to the threat of nuclear war with the Soviet Union and the need to stop arms control efforts, to develop a "war winning" strategy, and to build up enough weapons to assure U.S. nuclear superiority. The CPD was very supportive of policies that required the acquisition of enormous quantities of new hardware. The nuclear war fighting policies alone called for over 100 billion dollars in B-1 bombers, 50 billion dollars in new submarines and related procurements, 50 to 100 billion dollars in MX missiles, and hundreds of billions of dollars in research and development and hardware for a ballistic missile defense system that could ultimately cost more than one trillion dollars (Axelrod, Schwartz, and Boies 1986).

The CPD's political emphasis on supporting policy changes requiring huge investments in new hardware indicates that the most measurable effect observers are likely to see resulting from CPD political activity is enlarged military expenditures. Moreover, these expenditure increases should be apparent in almost all major categories of hardware, but less apparent (if present at all) in non-hardware areas like ammunition, chemicals, and operations and maintenance. I hypothesize that high levels of CPD activity will significantly increase expenditures in most categories of hardware. Figure 3.1 diagrams this hypothesis. Edsall (1984), Ferguson and Rogers (1981, 1986) and Himmelstein (1990) suggest the three variables on the left-hand side of the model as potential causes of the large scale New Right Social Movement, in which the CPD is deeply embedded.

These authors, however, do not specifically discuss whether these general factors contributed to the formation of the CPD and the research I present here does not test these authors' hypotheses concerning the formation of the New Right. There are two key points to note in this model. During the pre-1980 period the CPD attempted to exert influence on the state through lobbying and other tactics from the outside of the state; but, with the election of Reagan in 1980, many of the founders and higher visibility members of the CPD (many of whom had other roles in the New Right Social Movement) became members of the state management cadre. Once this transformation occurs the social movement begins to exert its influence directly through the structures of the state from within the state apparatus. The key link in this model that I focus my data analysis on is between the CPD political activity and changes in military expenditures.[10]

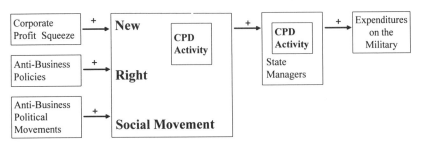

Figure 3.1. Model the Relationship between Elite Social Movement Activity and Weapons Expenditures

It is noteworthy that during the period covered by my data on military expenditures, 1962 through 1986, the Committee on the Present Danger and the New Right Social Movement were unique events. This poses some difficult empirical and theoretical problems for my research. Simply finding a correlation between CPD activity and the expansion of military expenditures would not rule out the chance that the observed relationship was coincidental and, therefore, spurious. This problem is ubiquitous to any project that examines the role of a one-time phenomenon like a social movement, war, or other similar historical occurrence. However, I have done several things that reduce the likelihood that any relationships between CPD activity and expenditures are spurious. Rather than use a simple dummy variable representing the period when the CPD was active, I use a variable approximating the rise and fall of the organization's political action over its life span. Therefore, if this variable fits the data well the likelihood of simple coincidence is low. Additionally, because I use multiple measures of military expenditures, a significant effect for the CPD measure across a range of expenditure variables would militate against coincidence. While I use the model shown in figure 3.1 to guide my data analysis, based on the results I present in chapter 5, I examine a number of alternative models concerning the role the CPD and the New Right played in determining procurement expenditures.

4

THEORIES OF THE STATE AND THE MILITARY

State-Oriented Approaches to the Study of Military Spending

THE DOMINANT BODY of scholarship examining questions of military spending and budgeting posits at least some autonomy of the central state from groups and organizations within civil society (Frankel 1979). This literature ranges from the case studies of weapons system that focus on decisions surrounding individual weapons systems (e.g., Cobb 1968) to the macro-oriented Marxist studies of the relationship between the structure of society to the behavior of the state, such as the work of James O'Connor (1973). The key common component of this body of scholarship is its focus on the structure of the state, especially the executive branch of the U.S. government, as the important determinant of policy formation.

Frankel (1979) suggests two basic groupings of theoretical perspectives in this diverse group of literature. The first and most prevalent approach that I examine here concerns the state politics models. This approach overlaps considerably with the more general pluralist model of the state. The second approach includes the Marxist models consisting of the work of the Marxist-structuralists, such as O'Connor (1973), Offe and Ronge (1979) and Poulantzas (1973, 1972), and the monopoly capital theorists, such as Baran and Sweezy (1966). This latter body of scholarship mixes many of the ideas of the

Marxist-structuralists with some central ideas common to Marxist-instrumentalists.

The central difference between the state politics models and the Marxist approaches lies in their treatment of the state decision process. To the state politics theorists, the key to understanding state policy output is the organizational structure and process of the state. This theory focuses almost entirely on causes internal to the organs of the state. Indeed, recent contributions by sociologists who work in this perspective present the military as being the bureaucracy most autonomous from the rest of society as well as from the majority of the rest of state apparatus (Hooks 1991). The Marxist model, on the other hand, looks to the structure of the economy to derive the likely policy activities of the state. These scholars hypothesize root causes external to the state apparatus. The state decisions, however, are usually rationally reactive to the environment and can remain relatively autonomous from external politics of almost every type. In the case of the monopoly capital model, however, the political activities of capitalists and labor play an important role in constraining the autonomy of the state.

State Politics

Within this model there are two very similar ways of examining the functioning of the state: the budgetary politics approach that is common in political science and the state-centered approach that is common in sociology. The budgetary politics approach is, by far, the most commom in the literature concerning the military. In contrast, sociologists guided by state-centered theory have concentrated on the welfare state (e.g., Weir, Orloff, and Skocpol 1988; Skocpol and Orloff 1984; and Skocpol 1980). An important exception to this trend, however, is the recent work of Gregory Hooks on the formation of the post–World War II warfare state (1990a, 1991).

Aaron Wildavsky (1984) gives an excellent survey of the primary features of the bureaucratic politics approach, the central component of the state politics perspective. The major actors identified by Wildavsky's and other's research include the major congressional oversight committees—in the case of the military the focus is on Senate and House armed services committees—and the executive branch, especially the Office of Management and Budget, Office of the Secretary of Defense, and the various service branches (Ball 1980; Kanter 1975; Lucas and Dawson 1974; Halperin 1972; Cobb 1968; Huntington 1961). In this literature the primary variables explaining defense spending decisions are either interorganizational competition or intraorganizational interests and procedures. External forces come into play only when there is a major crisis such as war or when there is a large scale force at work leading to budget cutting or spending moods in Congress or the Office of the President (Wildavsky 1984).[1] Most researchers using this approach implicitly or explicitly exclude from their work any significant analysis of the causes of these major crises or changes in mood and rarely indicate the process through which these phenomena change the behavior of the state. This focus on complex organizational procedures and conflicts leads the vast majority of researchers using bureaucratic politics models to conclude that, unless there are exceptional circumstances, nearly all decisionmaking is incremental.

One obvious problem with the narrow focus on internal organizational process and structure is that no theory of the sources of external events of significance is inherent to the model, despite its reliance on exceptionalism to explain major changes in bureaucratic behavior. Indeed, to explain some decision outcomes researchers rely heavily on this escape clause. For example, Beard (1976) in his research on the development of ICBMs and the United States' civilian space program portrays the launch by the Soviet Union of Sputnik as a very important, but only superficially examined, cause of a number of major changes in missile development programs in the United States. He does this because the launch of Sputnik was an exceptional occurrence and thus not relevant to his development of a bureaucratic politics model of U.S. military and civilian missile programs. Beard made no attempt to examine why the Soviets launched Sputnik, why they were the first nation to send a satellite into orbit, or even why Sputnik had such an important effect on U.S. policymakers. Major changes in policy are not explained by well-integrated theory, but rather by viewing such events as exceptions to the theory and outside the bounds of the current discussion.

The logic of the bureaucratic model indicates a number of variables of interest to the study of military budgets. The most important is last year's budget (Ostrom 1977). The ubiquitous incrementalism common in massive bureaucracies like the U.S. military as well as the high likelihood of any time series analysis being unable to measure all important variables (Johnston 1984; Judge et al. 1980) usually make last year's budget the most important variable in any time series analysis focusing on budgets and expenditures.

Budgetary theorists view the formal structure of the rules and regulations governing the budgetary process, especially those rules that apply to the various bureaucracies, as the key component influencing budgetary decisionmaking (Korb 1981; 1977; Coulam 1977). Of particular interest to research examining the military has been the effects of planned-program budgeting, zero-based budgeting (ZBB), and management-by-objectives budgeting on policy outcomes. Despite being proclaimed as ways to hold government spending in check (Wildavsky 1984), the extant research in the area does not provide much quantitative evidence supporting widespread effects of the different budgetary process reforms on levels of spending (for example, see Korb 1981).

Organizational competition is another central feature of the budgetary politics model. Research on budgetary politics often concludes that the interaction of the self-interest of members of the bureaucracies with the self-interest of the organizations is a major determinant of bureaucratic behavior and, therefore, policy output (Wildavsky 1984). In the area of the military, the central competition is among the different branches of the service over goals and missions, budgetary allocations, weapons design inputs, and a host of lesser aspects of policy. The role of interservice rivalries in military decisionmaking is one of the most widely accepted patterns of bureaucratic behavior examined by research using the bureaucratic politics model. Despite its acceptance, attempts at the quantification of this phenomenon are rare, especially regarding this variable's impact on levels of expenditures. The majority of the research finding this behavior is from case studies of weapons systems (for example, see Beard 1976; Cobb 1968). Kanter's (1975) research using the number of reports of dissenting Joint Chiefs of Staff as a measure of bureaucratic competition is one of the few attempts at quantifying

78

the effects of interservice rivalries on decisions shaping White House military policy.

One possible reason for the lack of quantitative investigations examining interservice rivalries is that the majority of the extant literature suggests that this phenomenon is present in nearly all military-related decision processes. This limited variation makes it very difficult to quantitatively assess the impact of interservice rivalry on decision outcomes. Moreover, the literature indicates that not only is bureaucratic competition relatively constant, but its main influence is on micro aspects of weapons decisions, for example, do we go with the 96-inch Air Force design for the MX missile or the Navy's 84-inch diameter common missile design (Holland 1985). The competition among the various parts of the armed services is rarely touted by these scholars as being the primary explanation of more macro decisions such as general force levels and the allocation of expenditures into general categories of weapons, except in the broadest of terms.

Large-scale bureaucratic competition in the form of conflicts among large groups of bureaucratic entities is easier for quantitative researchers to tackle. The dominant large-scale competition relevant here is between the welfare state and the military, often referred to as the "guns versus butter" competition. Domke et al. (1983) examined this potential competition among a number of western democracies including the United States but found little empirical support for the presence of this level of competition.

One extension of the bureaucratic politics model concerns how the electoral process influences state policy (Tufte 1978). The focus of this research is primarily on the use by incumbents of the powers of office to manipulate policy outcomes to increase their popularity during election years. It is important to realize that this perspective is largely an add-on to other research (e.g., Griffin, Devine, and Wallace 1982a, 1982b). Essentially, these authors suggest that a president or members of Congress will try to increase spending on defense just before an election as a way to reduce unemployment and otherwise improve economic conditions. This will supposedly make it more likely that incumbents will be reelected. Most researchers measure the meaningful processes of this approach with simple dichotomous variables for the presence of an election year (usually presidential election years), majority party in the House or Senate, and party of the President (Griffin, Devine, and Wallace 1982b; Nincic and Cusock 1978). Griffin, Devine, and Wallace (1982a), as well as other authors, suggest that military expenditure levels should be likely to rise during the last year of a presidential term, especially if there are high rates of unemployment during the president's term in office.

Of lesser importance to this model is the ideological difference between major parties as another influence on policy (Greenstein 1977). For example, some authors suggest that some administrations, such as the Carter administration, were committed to low levels of defense spending, while others, such as the Reagan administration, because of the nature of their class constituencies, were oriented to higher weapons expenditures (Himmelstein and Clawson 1984; Shoup 1980; Sale 1976). However, to date there are no quantitative examinations of this specific hypothesis.

A recent addition to the debates surrounding the role of the state in modern society that is closely related to the budgetary politics model is the research of the state-centered theorists originating with the work of Theda Skocpol (1980; see also Weir, Orloff, and Skocpol 1988; Skocpol and Orloff 1984).[2] Broadly, there are six primary contentions common to the scholars who call themselves state-centered theorists that are relevant to this book.

1. The state is autonomous from the rest of society except in times of major social upheaval such as revolution (Skocpol 1980; 1979).
2. The state does, however, respond to external forces, but only forces external to the society as well, for example, international economic, military, and political competition (Hooks 1990; Skocpol 1979).
3. The nature of preexisting state institutions and bureaucracies, as well as their capacities, largely determines the extent and shape of new policies, programs, and institutions as well as the evolution of existing organs of the state (Orloff and Skocpol 1984).
4. State managers, people in control of state bureaucracies, as well as some types of elected officials and high level political appointees, control the organs of the state.

5. The decisions of state managers are guided by the interests of the state, the bureaucracies they control, and their own self-interests (Hooks 1990a; 1990b; 1991; Weir, Orloff, and Skocpol 1988).

6. An additional conditioning force in the behavior of the state is the nature of political parties and their role in policymaking through Congress and the Office of the President (Skocpol and Ementa 1986; Orloff and Skocpol 1984; Skocpol 1980).[3]

With only one exception, sociologists using this state-centered model concentrate on the initiation and process of the modern welfare state, especially New Deal legislation. Hooks (1991; 1990) is the only sociologist who has applied this approach to the military. His primary research explores the formation of the "military state" during World War II and the role that the military buildups during and after World War II had on state formation and economic change. The work of Hooks that is most central to the discussion here is his analysis of the rearmament of the United States that began in 1949 (1990). Hooks's central findings include: the state is able to dominate the defense industry—indeed, Hooks concludes that the Pentagon is autarkic; the state is strong enough to carry out industrial planning on a large scale;[4] the national security interests of the state as articulated by state managers largely residing in the Pentagon (mainly high-ranking military officers) drove the post-war rearmament; and the interests and political activities of groups outside the state, especially capitalists, had no impact on the process or the ultimate form of the military state.

To Hooks the primary force behind the contemporary military is national security. Pentagon planners, mostly uniformed, react rationally to threats to the United States' national interest when dictating weapons purchases, research and development expenditures, and military force deployment. Unfortunately, Hooks does not provide a definition of national security or national interest that is useful for generating empirical operationalizations and hypotheses. Instead, Hooks states,

During and after World War II, the strategic posture of the United States shifted from defense (i.e., preventing foreign powers from conquering the

United States) to national security, that includes the protection of U.S. economic, political, and military interests throughout the world (McLauchlan 1988; Leffler 1984). In this all-encompassing definition of U.S. interests, "virtually every development in the world is perceived to be potentially crucial" (Yergin 1977:196) and requires ongoing military preparedness. (1990:366)

It is surprising that, despite the centrality of the causes of changes in U.S. military policy to Hooks's argument about the power of the state vis-à-vis defense contractors, he uses an ambiguous definition of national security, one that is virtually impossible to operationalize or evaluate. More importantly, in part because of the ambiguity of his operationalization of national security, he never directly demonstrates that national security is *the* causal force behind U.S. military policy. Instead, Hooks attempts to demonstrate that because defense firms are more dependent for resources on the Pentagon than the Pentagon is on defense contractors, the interests of individual defense firms play no role in the allocation of defense resources. By process of elimination, national security must, therefore, be the central force behind U.S. military policy. This approach makes it problematic for the empirical researcher to establish testable measures of national security policy to evaluate competing theoretical explanations.

The state-centered theory emphasizes the effect of existing institutional formations on future policy and programs. This indicates that, at its core, state-centered theory has something very much in common with the budgetary politics model of Aaron Wildavsky. More specifically, Hooks's operationalization of national security emphasizes large-scale and long-term commitments by the state to military programs that include not only the initial buildup of a large and powerful military force, but the rational maintenance and modernization of that force (for discussions of rationality and defense planning, see Gansler 1989; Collins 1982, 1978). Furthermore, the national security issues, which from this perspective are seen to determine military policy, are so broad that only in extreme cases would military procurement policy be immediately reactive to the behavior of other nations, most especially the old Soviet Union.[5] Therefore, the central empirical relationship concerning military expenditures emphasized by the state-centered approach to the military is that last year's expenditure levels should be a consistent predictor of the current year's expenditures, except in cases of unusual and major national security threats or significant social or political change. This hypothesis is little different from Wildavsky's budgetary politics model, although there is some divergence on the reasons for this proposed relationship.

In summary, the state politics approach to studying the military is remarkable in the variety of substantive and methodological subjects it embraces. The primary idea that encompasses the wide range of research found in this perspective is that the central actors in propelling state policy are people who hold positions with the state, elected, appointed, or otherwise employed. The interests of state managers, the interests of the organizations employing them, and the structure of rules and regulations guiding the individual's and bureaucracy's behavior are the ultimate sources of state policy output. The state-centered model adds to this theme the role of resources and capacities residing in the organs of the state as significant determinants of the behavior of the state. The central quantitatively testable hypothesis generated by both strains of the state politics approach is that next year's budgetary expenditures will be dependent on this year's expenditures, barring significant social, economic, or political changes. Short-term fluctuations in expenditure levels are likely to be the result of changes in the bureaucratic process governing a given expenditure area, the electoral cycle, the winning of bureaucratic competitions by one or more bureaucracies, and the ideological makeup of electoral bodies such as the legislature.

Marxist Models

Marxist scholars apply two somewhat different, but directly related, models to the military in the United States. Monopoly capital models posit a special political and structural link between capital and labor in the monopoly sector of the United States economy and the federal government.[6] The second prevalent approach is the Marxist-structuralist model derived from Marx's writings by theoreticians such as Nicos Poulantzas (1972, 1973), O'Connor (1973), and Offe and Ronge (1982). These models mostly differ from the monopoly capital arguments in their emphasis on the relative autonomy of the state. This perspective maintains that the state can only be relatively autonomous from the political behavior of social-class relations because both are part of the mode of production (Poulantzas 1978; Prechel 1990:562).

The monopoly capital argument centers on the late capitalist economy's problem with economic surplus. The modern capitalist economy can absorb this surplus in many ways, for example, "improved sales and marketing techniques, [and] epoch-making inventions" (Griffin et al. 1982a). However, the role of military spending in absorbing this surplus is considered unique by Baran and Sweezy (1966). This type of large expenditure is the most politically acceptable to both capital and labor, especially in the monopoly sector. It offers a relatively direct and efficient way for money to be transferred from the state to capitalists and then to organized labor. Moreover, many parts of the military budget, particularly expenditures on procurement, can be manipulated relatively easily from year to year and sometimes from quarter to quarter. Finally, military expenditures can pay for something of direct profitmaking value to capital, a military machine capable of expanding and protecting the foreign investment and trade networks necessary to many monopoly capital firms' profits (O'Connor 1973; Baran and Sweezy 1966). Welfare expenditures, as well as most other non-military expenditures, do not have this double-barreled support of the accumulation process.

Another central component of this body of theory is that the state is both especially dependent on the monopoly sector of the economy for taxes and political support and is most heavily influenced by the needs of capitalists and their enterprises in this sector of the economy compared to other portions of society. Thus, while the monopoly capital model suggests that the state is more autonomous than does the Marxist-instrumentalist model, it also hypothesizes special political and economic linkages between the monopoly sector of the economy and the central state. A central difference, therefore, between the monopoly capital theorists and the Marxist-structuralists is that the former emphasize the existence of political activities (broadly defined) as an important mechanism through which the needs of capital are turned into policy. This difference is one of the reasons the monopoly capital model emphasizes the importance of the interests of the monopoly capital sector of the economy to state decisionmaking while the more structuralist arguments tend to be more widely encompassing of all sectors of the economy.

The relevant outcome of the special dependency between the state and the monopoly capital sector of the economy is that the state is empowered to manage the economy by using available politically acceptable tools at hand, most especially Keynesian economic principles. The use of the military budget for Keynesian countercyclical policy beginning in the late 1940s was the result of ". . . a coalition of organized labor, monopoly capitalists, and cold warriors, among other groups that prevailed in late 1940s politics" (Gold, 1977 quoted in Griffin, Devine, and Wallace 1982b). Thus, the monopoly capital adherents, as well as the rest of the Marxist structuralists, would argue that the U.S. federal government will increase the military budget in times of economic crisis and reduce it when the economy's health improves.

The crisis of underconsumption and overproduction is also the focus of the pure structuralists. They also argue that the state must manage the polity and economy of capitalist society to maintain the profits of capital, especially capital in the monopoly sector (O'Connor 1973). They even posit the same tools as the monopoly capital theorists, Keynesian monetary and fiscal policy. Scholars in this camp also consider military expenditures to be the most politically acceptable and, therefore, most legitimate way for the state to stimulate the economy (O'Connor 1973). The primary difference between these scholars lies mostly in their identification of sources of state autonomy. The monopoly capital scholars posit that constraints on state autonomy lie in the political machinations of a particular group, a coalition of capital and labor in the monopoly sector of the economy. On the other hand the structuralists argue that while the political machinations of social classes and class segments do constrain the state, the state's dependence on the economy for taxes and legitimacy requires the state to act to alleviate impending economic crises even when it is not in the interests (perceived or otherwise) of individual capitalists (Offe and Ronge 1979; Miliband 1977; O'Connor 1973). The use of military expenditures by the state to alleviate crises of capitalism stems from its high degree of political appeal to capitalists and labor as well as its apparent efficacy.

It is very important to realize that whatever difference these two approaches might have concerning the exact nature of state autonomy, they both posit the same types of outcomes from essentially the same causes. Inherent structural contradictions in late capitalist economies, specifically the crises of underconsumption and overproduction, must be managed by the state through Keynesian countercyclical economic policy. The mechanism of choice is military expenditure.[7] It offers a politically acceptable and relatively direct and efficient way to pump money into the pockets of capital. Furthermore, military expenditure has an obvious use value to capital because it supports a military machine capable of expanding and protecting the foreign investment made by U.S. firms that is an increasingly important source of capital accumulation.[8]

Griffin, Devine, and Wallace (1982a, 1982b) apply the monopoly model to quantitative data on the U.S. military. Their work examines the monopoly capital thesis while controlling for a number of additional variables suggested by other models including the budgetary politics models. The key monopoly capital measures tested by Griffin and his colleagues are monopoly sector corporate profits (as well as change in these profits from one year to the next), unionized sector unemployment rates, manufacturing sector unemployment rates, overall rates of economic concentration, and a dummy variable coded 1 for a recession year. The most robust effects found by these authors on the percentage share of U.S. gross national product (GNP) devoted to defense expenditures are union employment and percent change in monopoly sector profits. The authors interpret this as indicating support for a "modified" monopoly capital theory of state policy development that makes explicit links between unionized unemployment and military Keynesianism (Griffin, Devine, and Wallace 1982b:S113).

Recent sociological work takes issue with the theoretical link between the interests of the monopoly sector and defense expenditures by claiming that defense sales and defense contracts are concentrated in a restricted set of client firms that are not really part of the monopoly sector of the U.S. economy (Hooks 1990:362). This position overlooks data indicating that many monopoly sector firms receive large defense contracts that, very importantly, often contribute a disproportionate share of profits to the firm. For example, Chrysler Corporation's M-1 Abrahms tank production subsidiary was the only subsidiary contributing substantial profit to the firm during the early 1980s. In 1957 and 1958 fifty-three non-defense dependent monopoly sector firms were among the largest one hundred defense contractors. These firms received about 27 percent of all defense contracts, about $5.1 billion, and just one year later the proportion of contract awards to monopoly sector firms had grown to 34 percent (U.S. Office of the Secretary of Defense 1959, 1958). More significantly, monopoly capital is indirectly connected through substantial stock ownership of defense corporations by monopoly sector capitalists, industrial corporations, and large financial firms as well as by receiving subcontracts from the prime military contractors. In the period from 1959 through 1962, non-defense firms acquired 137 defense contractors. Firms located primarily in either the fabricated metals industry or in non-electrical machinery acquired 62 of these defense contractors. Every major industry group except tobacco and leather products made an acquisition in the defense industry (Nathanson 1969). Moreover, metals, chemicals, food, and most of the inputs into defense sector production or normal defense operations come from firms in the monopoly sector. For example, from 1956 through 1974, seven to nineteen oil companies, including most of the major oil companies, were among the top 100 defense contractors. Hence, there is no reason to believe that the monopoly sector of the economy does not directly and indirectly benefit from defense procurement expenditures.

One of the key reasons for the political acceptability of military expenditures as a tool of economic management is its significant use function to capital in maintaining conditions necessary for profitable foreign investment (Baran and Sweezy 1966; especially O'Connor 1973:153). Therefore, it is reasonable to expect that military spending should respond not just to the economic health of monopoly capital in the United States, but also to threats to its health from overseas. In addition, the evidence indicates that since the turn of the century, overseas U.S. business interests have been deeply institutionalized in our government's foreign policy apparatus (Roy 1981, 1977). Moreover, considering the increasing share of U.S. firms' investment that is going abroad, the value of capital's overseas interests to the health of monopoly firms should prove to be increasingly important in determining the allocation of expenditures to the military (and probably within the military) regardless of the general health of the U.S. economy. Despite research on the Keynesian countercyclical hypothesis by a number of scholars (for example, Alex Mintz and Beth Hicks [1984] report additional support for this hypothesis), this aspect of the monopoly capital model has not been quantitatively examined.

Variables Derived from State Autonomy Models of Military Expenditures

The budgetary process, state-centered, and Marxist models suggest that several groups of variables are important for explaining the allocation of military expenditures. The budgetary process model proposes that measures of bureaucratic inertia, organizational competition, organizational structure, and electoral politics are important forces at work shaping government policy. The state-centered approach would also indicate that these variables are important (see Hooks 1991b; 1990; Skocpol and Orloff 1984; Skocpol 1980).[9] The structuralist approach focuses on problems of underconsumption and overproduction inherent in the capitalist economy. The monopoly capital model focuses specific attention on underconsumption crises in the monopoly sector of the economy. Thus, both Marxist models support using measures of economic conditions for capital and labor in both the monopoly sector of the economy and in the whole economy. The role of overseas investment described by Baran and Sweezy leads me to examine a measure of the value of foreign investment to capital in the United States.

State Politics Model

Because of the difficulty of finding an appropriate measure of inter-service rivalry, I do not attempt to determine the influence of this dimension of budgetary politics on the distribution of military expenditures. My reading of the literature suggests that no potential measure was manageable given the existing quantitative data. However, it is possible to examine the variable most central to the budgetary process approach—current expenditures lagged one year. Because military expenditures of all types have, with few exceptions, experienced an overall growth in real terms since the beginning of the time series used here (1962) until near its end (1986),[10] the expected effect of this variable is that last year's expenditures should have a uniform positive influence on all categories of military expenditures.

The postulated role of the formal structure of the budgetary process has primarily been examined in qualitative research such as Lawrence J. Korb's analysis of three systems of budgeting (1977). During the period covered by my data the federal government only applied zero-based budgeting and the newer reforms under the Congressional Budgetary Reform Act beginning in 1976 to the Department of Defense budgetary process (Wildavsky 1984). I use a dummy variable coded 0 for the ZBB period and 1 for the period beginning in 1976 when the new budgetary reforms were first instituted. Proponents of these reforms have claimed significant budgetary reductions resulting from the creation of the Congressional Budgetary Office in 1976 and other concurrent reforms. Edmund Muskie, then chairman of the Senate Budget Committee, for example, stated that the new reforms saved over $15 billion in fiscal year 1977 (Muskie 1976). Thus I expect that this dummy variable for budgetary reform should have a uniform negative influence across all categories of expenditures. However, for some categories of expenditures, such as ships, the contract commitments are for such a long time that there might be no measurable effect of budgetary reforms for many years. Thus, there may be no significant relation in my data for such categories as ships and missiles.

Because of the complexity of the role of electoral politics in determining military expenditures I use a number of measures to examine this relationship. I measure the effect of political party in power with a dummy coded 1 for years when a Republican president is in office and 0 otherwise as do Griffin, Devine, and Wallace (1982b). Additionally, I use the number of Democratic senators and Democratic members of the House of Representatives on expenditures and the ratio of Democrats to Republicans in both the House and the Senate as independent variables in my analysis.

Another electoral factor suggested by the work of Griffin and his colleagues as being a potentially important determinant of military spending is the self-interest of incumbents. These scholars posit that incumbents may use the state to improve economic conditions to improve their overall popularity with the electorate. In this analysis I use the same variable appearing in Griffin, Devine and Wallace (1982b), a dummy coded 1 for a presidential election year, 0 otherwise.

An officeholder's popularity with the electorate has increasingly become important to contemporary politics. This is largely because the President and his or her office can use high levels of general popularity with the electorate as a source of political power over Congress and other potential competitors. Thus, I submit that besides manipulating defense expenditures to give a boost to the economy before or during an election year, an incumbent may use these mechanisms to boost or maintain his or her popularity to obtain or retain political hegemony. Therefore, I expect that declining presidential popularity should result in increasing expenditures. Because large and showy military activities are most likely to significantly increase popularity (activities such as invading Grenada, bombing Libya, or destroying the Iraqi army), the effect of this variable should be especially evident in the area of operations and maintenance, the source of many of the funds for unbudgeted military operations. I assay the potential influence of a presidential administration's popularity with the mid-year percentage approval rating of the job the President is doing published by Gallup Incorporated.

Figure 4.1 provides a general illustration of the state politics model. In this model last year's expenditures has a positive and strong effect on next year's expenditures on the military, especially for the most aggregated levels of military expenditures. Electoral politics

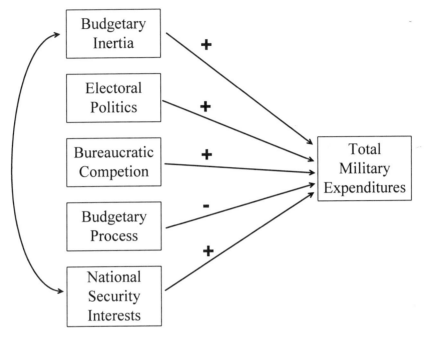

Figure 4.1. Simplified Model of the State Politics Approach

and bureaucratic competition are likely to result in increases in spending during certain periods of the election cycle and budgetary cycle. Reforms and other changes in the budgetary process should reduce all types of expenditures. It is important to emphasize here that these processes occur within the state. It is state managers, essentially autonomous from the political machinations of social classes and other groups, who are competing for resources, manipulating the electorate, following regulations, and building on previous organizational structures.

A final aspect of the state politics approach is the influence of the state-centered theorist's version of national security interests, as defined by state managers, on military expenditures. The complex processes of turning national security interests into military expenditures manifest themselves in a simple relationship, last year's expenditures largely determine this year's expenditures. This is the same empirical prediction given by budgetary process models.

Variables Derived from the Monopoly Capital Model

The monopoly capital model focuses primarily on the use of military expenditures to manage the health of the economy. Furthermore, the most prominent research postulates a sector-specific class coalition model (Baran and Sweezy 1966; Griffin, Devine, and Wallace 1982a; 1982b). This added complexity of the monopoly capital approach, as well as the relative ambiguity of the concepts of economic performance and crisis, indicates that any research using this model must include a wide range of measures of economic structure and performance.

An important difference between the research I present here and past research examining economic influences on military expenditures is that the primary dependent variables in this study are military expenditures disaggregated into several categories of expenditures. Previous research has almost entirely used aggregate expenditures on the military or aggregate military procurement expenditures. Consequently, I expect the results of this analysis to diverge in several ways from previous research. Because the monopoly capital model states that the behavior of the monopoly sector of the economy is a central influence on Keynesian countercyclical resource allocation by the state, using disaggregated expenditures data may show sharpened effects of economic measures on some categories of spending. For many expenditure categories, such as armored vehicles and aircraft, a few firms in an even smaller number of industry sectors at the core of the monopoly sector of the economy (transportation, aerospace, and motor vehicles) receive the majority of expenditures. For other categories such as ammunition and operations and maintenance the expenditures go to more and smaller firms in a wider range of industry sectors, many of which are in the competitive sector. Therefore, I expect to see stronger effects for the measures of monopoly sector economic performance in expenditure categories linked to monopoly sector firms than in others, specifically the categories of missiles, ships, aircraft, tanks, communications, and electronics.

Another divergence of significance between this research and previous research examining the impact of economic variables on the military is that this research uses the absolute amount of expenditures in constant dollars for each year rather than the percentage of U.S. GNP spent on the military used by others. Moreover, researchers such as Griffin and his colleagues use current dollars in calculating their dependent variables. This procedure could produce misleading results because military expenditures and procurement have rates of inflation that differ markedly from the GNP; for example, the price deflator for military procurement sometimes increases twice as fast as the GNP deflator (U.S. Department of Commerce 1987). Thus, in many of the years in their time series Griffin and his colleagues very well might not have been modeling changes in the commitment of resources to the military as they thought, but rather differences in the rates of inflation for the GNP and for military expenditures. The time series I use here also encompasses a more recent period than does previous research. Almost without exception, no work using the monopoly capital model has used a series with data more recent than 1981. The series used here ends in 1987 for most data.

The measures I use for the key independent variables from the monopoly capital model are similar to those used by Griffin and his colleagues. A key group of these variables includes the corporate net profit after taxes for the chemical, petroleum, primary nonferrous (mostly aluminum), primary ferrous, electrical machinery, transportation, and motor vehicle industries (all from the U.S. Department of Commerce 1987). These measures of profits should behave differently for different categories of expenditure if the Keynesian based decisionmaking penetrates beyond simply setting the aggregate levels of arms expenditures. To look at aggregate monopoly sector profits I excerpted a time series from Dumenil, Glick, and Rangel (1987) containing the rate of corporate profits before taxes on gross replacement cost of capital in the manufacturing sector for 1962 to 1986.[11] To examine the labor side of the monopoly capital argument I use manufacturing unemployment and the more specific manufacturing unemployment in durable goods industries.

The Marxist-structuralist models of military Keynesianism do not always hypothesize any special importance to the monopoly sector. To these authors more general measures of the state of capitalist profits spur Keynesian countercyclical policies. Thus, in this analysis I also assayed the effects of corporate profits adjusted for capital consumption, income from dividends, and income from interest. Since declining profits are likely to be a cause of businesses failing, I also included the total number of business failures per year and the number of business failures per 100,000 businesses for each year (all from the U.S. Department of Commerce 1987).

An important, but yet unexamined, aspect of the monopoly capital model is the role of overseas interests in military expenditure decisionmaking. One measure of overseas interest that seems to get at the heart of capitalist concerns with international markets is the total net profit from U.S.-owned assets abroad (U.S. Department of Commerce 1987). This variable measures the impact of overseas capital on its owners' profits in the United States rather than just the book value of foreign investments or similar measure. The book value of foreign assets or like measures can be misleading because they are heavily dependent on factors such as exchange rates, taxation definitions, and takeover bids. I posit that the more profit coming from overseas investments, the more valuable that investment becomes to U.S. capital. This should spur state managers in the U.S. government to spend more on protecting these interests as part of its world police role and it seems it would spur capitalists to agitate for more expenditures to protect those increasingly valuable interests. Because one of the most significant threats to overseas investments comes from political instability and revolution in lesser developed nations, it seems likely that categories of expenditures for weapons most useful in these situations should respond particularly well to changes in this variable. The categories showing the strongest effects are likely to be aircraft, ships, and operations and maintenance. Figure 4.2 illustrates the relationship between U.S. corporate interests abroad and military expenditures as well as the influence monopoly sector economic health has on military expenditures.

Monopoly sector economic health has the effect of increasing military expenditures when the profitability of monopoly sector corporations is low or declining, but once the economy is healthy, state

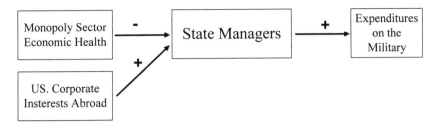

Figure 4.2 Simplified Model of Monopoly Capital Model

managers are free to return to reduced spending levels. It is important to note that in some theories proposing these types of relationships the role of state managers is to manage the economy for capitalists, regardless of what capitalists might think they want (for example, Offe and Ronge 1982). Therefore, it is irrelevant who makes up the cadre of managers. Theorists at the other end of the spectrum, however, would argue that one of the reasons the state takes the interests of capital so seriously is because the management cadre consists largely of capitalists and their hand-picked representatives (for example, Miliband 1969; Gold 1977). Regardless of these distinctions, the relationships proposed by the different camps remain essentially the same.

5

THE RESULTS

Data, Method, and Analysis

AT THE CORE of this analysis of military procurement are nine variables covering the annual expenditures made by the U.S. Department of Defense on two categories of supplies, ammunition, and chemicals, and seven categories of hardware, weapons (artillery, rifles, pistols), guided missiles (nuclear and nonnuclear, excluding warheads), aircraft (fixed-wing and helicopters), ships, armored vehicles, communications equipment, and electrical and electronic equipment. I selected these data series from over thirty categories listed in the Department of Defense publication *Prime Military Contract Awards by Service Category and Federal Supply Classification*. These nine categories of expenditures represent the majority of expenditures on procurement for all years available for this analysis. Despite the Government Printing Office's listing of this data source as first available in 1951, I was able to locate data only for 1962 to the present. The data used in this study are for 1962 through 1986.

I also include in this study time series data for three general types of defense expenditures for 1962 through 1986 from *The Statistical Abstract of the United States* and *The Annual Report of the Secretary of Defense*. These series are expenditures on research, development, testing and evaluation (RDT&E), operations and maintenance, and total procurement expenditures. Data for this last variable is only for 1962 through 1984. I used the price deflator for government

Table 5.1. Descriptive Statistics for Military Expenditures*

Variable	Mean	Skewness	Std. Dev.	Minimum	Maximum	N
Expenditures on Supplies						
Ammunition	1,536,600	1.369	989,830	538,100	4,121,000	24
Chemicals	78,037	1.964	65,696	33,320	271,190	24
Expenditures on Hardware						
Weapons	387,510	.224	196,240	123,000	707,200	24
Missiles	2,622,800	.960	761,550	1,545,000	4,353,000	24
Aircraft	4,949,200	.837	1,567,500	3,019,000	8,639,000	24
Ships	1,644,000	.167	653,140	473,100	3,218,000	24
Tanks	413,390	.096	206,280	101,900	765,600	24
Comm.	2,657,500	.825	1,051,200	1,333,000	5,168,000	24
Electronics	519,100	.306	166,390	286,700	824,300	24
Aggregate Expenditures						
RDT&E ($1 Mills)	8,621.0	.571	1,604.8	6,667	12,240	24
Operations & Maint ($1 Mills)	23,682	.500	3,961.8	18,330	31,630	24
Total Procurement ($100 mills)	778.52	.587	112.34	649.9	1005	22

*Values are in Thousands of 1972 Dollars except where noted.

purchases from *The Survey of Current Business* to convert all the data to 1972 dollars. This is one way to detrend this type of time series data and it ensures that the data for each year is comparable to every other year. The descriptive statistics presented in table 5.1 indicate that all of these dependent variables have distributions appropriate for ordinary least squares (OLS) regression.

A major concern in time series data analysis is the likelihood that autocorrelation will distort the results. I will examine techniques of detection and correction of autocorrelation later in this book. First, I want to examine several important limitations on my data that cannot be ameliorated by statistical technique. Perhaps the most important problem is that the primary data source, the U.S. Department of Defense, considers some aspects of the data classified. In *Prime Military Contract Awards by Service Category and Federal Supply Classification* a footnote states that data for some sub-categories of some supply categories are not the actual amounts spent but either reduced or inflated amounts.[1] The Directorate of Information, Operations, and Research adds or subtracts these differences to other sub-categories within the respective supply category such that totals for the supply categories still represent the actual amounts expended by the Department of Defense.

Fortunately, these manipulations only affect some sub-categories of procurement and then only for some years. The Directorate of Information (the organization that authors my primary data source) randomly selects which categories to manipulate. Thus, no systematic bias in the data is introduced, but the additional measurement error would attenuate any relationships that exist in the data. Because only subcategories of expenditures are the focus for these efforts of disinformation, the major categories remain unaffected by these machinations. Hence, because I only use the major categories of procurement, these Department of Defense security precautions do not influence the results I present in this book.

Another important limitation of this analysis is that I only use twenty-four years (lagging the variables reduces the number of cases by one) in my analysis. The period covered by the data excludes historical events that could be central to understanding the procurement process. Important events in the decade of the fifties that might have had significant effects on procurement processes, but are excluded from study, include the Korean War, a major economic slump, and the early stages of the development of new weapons technologies such as atomic and hydrogen bombs as well as long-range ballistic missiles. On the other hand, the period covered includes the peak of the Vietnam War and the arrival of strategic nuclear parity between the United States and the Soviet Union. One consequence of having only twenty-four years to work with is that the generalizability of estimates from the analyses might be open to question. However, the uniqueness of the included and excluded events is debatable. For example, while the disaggregated time series excludes the Korean War, it does include the Vietnam War. Economic slumps occur in both periods and major pushes by elite groups to increase arms expenditures also occur in both periods (for example, the CPD I and CPD II, see Sanders 1984). Still, the short period covered is problematic.

A final limitation is the lack of any readily available time series data on the former Soviet Union comparable to the disaggregated data used in this study. One consequence of this lack is that crossnational comparative analysis is not possible. While aggregated data series on the Soviet Union and its satellites similar to some of the aggregated United States data I use are available from the Department of State, the Department of Defense, and the Central Intelligence Agency, the validity and reliability of these data are suspect (Freedman 1986; Prados 1982). A second effect of not having a comparable data set to use is that I cannot acceptably perform tests of the very popular, but easily criticized, arms-race model of military procurement and decisionmaking (see Leidy and Staiger 1985; Nincic 1982; Richardson 1960 for reviews of this literature). Because of the paucity of comparable and good quality data on non-capitalist nations I make no attempt to generalize the results of this study to noncapitalist nations. Also, although my research does not examine the action–reaction theories, recent evidence suggests there is little empirical support for this model for the United States and the Soviet Union (Davis and Powell 1987; Griffin, Devine, Wallace 1982a; Nincic 1982; Nincic and Cusock 1979).

Despite the problems noted, analysis based on these data can, nevertheless, provide important new insight into arms purchasing in the United States and perhaps other capitalist nations as well. The disaggregated data give a far more detailed description of what military supplies the United States has purchased since 1962 than any other data set used by social scientists to date. These data begin to bridge the gap between the research using aggregate measures of military expenditures so common in the literature and the more common case study research. To date, researchers only use the quantitative analyses of U.S. military expenditures to examine the forces influencing the nation's commitment of resources to the military. Case studies have been the only source of information about how the Pentagon spends that money. The data I use here can increase our understanding of the forces influencing not only the resources committed to the military, but also the distribution of those resources among the different types of weapons and other kinds of expenditures.

The descriptive statistics for the independent measures used in this study presented in table 5.2 indicate no significant problems with nearly all measures. The distributions for annual war deaths, party of President, income from automobile manufacture, interest income, profits from manufacturing, and dividend income are somewhat skewed. I tested the effects of using the log of annual war deaths, profits from manufacturing, and dividend incomem as well as the square of income from auto manufacturing, on each of the expenditures variables (transformations suggested by Weisberg 1980). Party of President is a dummy variable and thus should not be transformed. Substituting these variables for their untransformed counterparts in the regression analysis produced no empirical reason to retain any of the transformed independent variables in the analysis.

This analysis examines the effects of twenty-two independent variables on twelve dependent variables. I did not simply estimate OLS equations with all twenty-two independent variables for each dependent measure because of the limited number of cases available and because of the likelihood that at least some of the independent variables are intercorrelated. Although other researchers examining military expenditures estimate large models with few cases (Griffin and his colleagues, for example, used as many as nine variables with as few as twenty-four cases in their published analysis), I do not do so for several reasons (Griffin, Devine, and Wallace, 1982b). Most

Table 5.2. Descriptive Statistics for Independent Variables Used in This Analysis*

Variable	Mean	Skewness	Std. Dev.	Minimum	Maximum	N
Earnings Per Share ($)	2.1842	.551	2.283	.4400	4.040	24
CPD Activity	.29600	.908	.40175	.00	1.00	24
1=Max. Activity						
Income From Assets Abroad ($1 Mills)	23,557	.345	12,522	8,600	44,180	24
Net Corp. Profit After Taxes From ($1 Mills):						
Nonferrous	890.27	-.414	661.99	-540.2	1,881	25
Chemicals	5,271.6	.024	1,640.9	2,669	7,764	25
Oil	8,246.9	.818	3,530.6	3,857	16,090	25
Transportation	1,261.6	.404	576.35	523.6	2,300	25
Cars	2,269.3	-4.042	4,995.7	-2,076	5,908	25
Ferrous	858.32	-1.189	1,317.8	-2,123	2,910	25
Interest Income ($100 mills)	1,483.9	3.123	1,557.4	345.6	8,090	25
Dividend Income ($100 Mills)	323.81	4.368	384.32	182.8	2,100	25
Rate of Profit, Mfg.	14.750	4.7555	.449	7.500	24.00	25
Manufacturing Unemp. (%)	6.475	.755	2.5062	3.20	12.30	25
Total Unemployment (%)	6.1360	.343	1.7407	3.5	9.7	25
Business Failures/100,000 firms	868.4	2.684	1,066.8	239	4,389	25
# Business Failures	2395.8	1.431	1,452.1	1,013	5,759	25
Party of President	1.56	4.600	.50662	1.00	2.00	25
1=Democrat						
2=Republican						
# Dems in House	263.36	.643	19.585	239.0	295.0	25
# Dems in Senate	59.040	.566	5.20	53.00	68.00	25
Election Year	.24000	1.193	.43589	.00	1.0	25
Presidential Popularity	50.900	-.159	13.135	25.00	75.00	25
Zero Based Budgeting Years	.16	1.817	.37417	.00	1.00	25
Annual War Deaths	1,855.2	2.128	3,835.5	.00	14,620	25

*Values are in Thousands of 1972 Dollars except where noted.

importantly, high ratios of independent variables to cases exacerbate the effects of multicollinearity. Too many independent variables also give artificially high goodness-of-fit measures; a problem exacerbated by autocorrelation. Finally, large regression models can be very difficult to interpret, even with large numbers of cases available (Kachigan 1982; Neter and Wasserman 1974).

The problems associated with the small sample size and the large number of independent variables required that variables unrelated to any measures described here be screened from the analysis. To determine what regression models to present I examined numerous regression models predicting the variables listed in table 5.2. Because of my small number of cases I could not use all the independent variables at the same time. Instead, I tested them in theory-determined groups and tested various subsets with variables I found to be statistically important predictors of at least two types of military procurement. None of the measures excluded from the tables of best regression models I present here had any noticeable effect on the observed relationships or had any statistically significant independent influence on the measures of procurement. This screening step selected only the measures of income from assets abroad, profit from ferrous metals, dividend income, manufacturing unemployment, CPD activity, and top defense contractors' earnings per share for additional analysis. Because other researchers have found war-related deaths to be a factor determining the amount of money spent by the military on both procurement and non-procurement budgetary items, I included the annual deaths resulting from the Vietnam War (from U.S. Department of Commerce 1972; 1978) as a control variable in all the regression analyses (Griffin, Devine, and Wallace 1982a, 1982b; Nincic 1982; Nincic and Cusock 1979).

The primary analytical tool used in this study is ordinary least squares regression. Because the data are a time series rather than a cross section of data, traditional regression techniques are likely to suffer from autocorrelated error terms, a ubiquitous and serious problem to the researcher using time series data (Judge, Griffiths, Hill, and Lee 1980; Winkler and Hays 1975). Autocorrelated residuals (also called serial correlation) is common with time series data because for many types of data collected over time, each observation is dependent on the previous observation. This can be due to certain types of measurement error, serially correlated variables not in the model being estimated, and from the nature of the processes creating the phenomenon being measured, for example, large slow-moving institutions creating budgets (Johnston 1984:309–310; Winkler and Hays 1975:713–714). The consequences of autocorrelation include inflated goodness-of-fit statistics such as R^2, inefficient estimates, and underestimates of the standard errors of the regression coefficients (Johnston 1984). Because the consequences of autocorrelation for OLS regression are so severe, it is paramount to detect any autocorrelation. Because I include the dependent variables lagged one year in all of my regression analyses, the most common of autocorrelation diagnostics, the Durbin-Watson statistic, is unsuitable (Godfrey 1978). Instead, I use the much more flexible Box-Pierce Q statistic and accompanying autocorrelation function and partial autocorrelation tables (based on the residuals from each regression equation) to detect the presence and form of any serial correlation among the residuals.[2] The corrections for indicated autocorrelation that were available for this analysis included the generalized least squares estimator to correct for first order moving average disturbances described by Harvey and McAvinchey (1981), the Prais-Winston algorithm for first order autoregressive disturbance, and a pseudo-difference algorithm developed by Greene (1988). I used SPSSX™ (SPSS Inc. 1988) and Limdep™ for the statistical analysis in this study (Greene 1989).

In this analysis I estimated separate regression models for each of the dependent variables. However, because these models, while computationally independent, are statistically dependent, there is a substantial likelihood that some of the statistically significant coefficients may be the result of chance. In the analysis presented here there are enough coefficients estimated that about five of the coefficients will have statistically significant t-tests (with $P < .05$) due to chance (Cliff 1987). The probability of making type I errors in the analysis increases. One way to correct for this likelihood is to use a simple Bonferoni correction that consists of multiplying the computer-calculated probability values of the t-tests of the coefficients by the number of dependent statistical tests, in this case 12. This will provide a probability value corrected for the number of dependent tests. The alpha level itself can also be corrected by dividing it by the number of dependent tests. For the data I present here, this indicates that a probability of .0042 is equivalent to an alpha of .05 for a single statistical test (Rosenthal and Rosnow 1987). This latter approach is the one I use in this book. There is, however, an important exception that many researchers make to this particular way of dealing with dependent statistical tests. In cases where there is a clear trend in the data, most researchers relax their application of the Bonferoni correction and will accept the uncorrected probability values as meaningful.

Results

Of the models presented in tables 5.3, 5.5, and 5.7, the only models benefiting from any corrections for autocorrelation were those predicting communications expenditures shown in tables 5.3 and 5.5. I used Green's pseudodifference algorithm to correct the detected serial correlation (Greene 1989). No model presented here benefited from either the application of Harvey and McAvinchey's moving average correction or Prais-Winston first-order autoregressive correction. The presence of some of the independent variables in some models produced autocorrelation that no amount of statistical manipulations could correct. The most problematic variables were war deaths, the two industry measures of corporate profits, manufacturing unemployment, and income from dividends. However, in all the models where these variables caused serious problems, the estimated coefficients were small and the t-tests of the coefficients indicated very large probability values (usually greater than .5).[3] Gross rate of profit in manufacturing also proved to be problematic in many models, most specifically in the models shown in table 5.3. This variable was less of a problem in the rest of the models, but none of the estimated coefficients for this variable were significant at the Bonferoni corrected alpha of .0042. In only three cases were the coefficients significant at the traditional alpha of .05. When I dropped these problematic variables from the models and lagged the dependent variables one year the Box-Pierce Q statistic and associated Box-Jenkins plots of the residuals showed no evidence of autocorrelated

Table 5.3. OLS Regression Coefficients from Best Models Estimating Procurement Expenditures from Committee on the Present Danger Activity, Earnings per Share, and Economic Measures While Controlling for Vietnam War Deaths with Corrections for Autocorrelation

Independent Variable	Chem.	Ammo.	Weapons	Guided Missiles	Aircraft	Ships	Armored Vehicles	Comm. DFR(1)#	Elect. Eqpt.	RDT&E	O&M	Total Proc.
Constant	−57,778.6	−137,752	−116,947	5,061,290	2,949,650	1,146,350	−440,429	739,453	257,419	−268.01	−61.058	727.46
	(.05663)[b]	(.09310)	(.23945)	(.00004)	(.00076)	(.00160)	(.78893)	(.22521)	(.00030)	(.82800)	(.97600)	(.00000)
Dept V_{T-1}	.88527	.152562	.224859	.068353	.479141	−.229315	−.368390	−c	−.024647	1.0110	.79469	—
	(.01259)	(.51755)	(.09400)	(.65281)	(.00153)	(.21889)	(.04220)		(.80368)	(.00000)	(.00000)	
Inc. from Assets Abroad	—	—	−2.36110	—	—	43.4793	15.0605	−49.6572	−6.16	−.00313	.02891	−.00967
			(.5182)			(.02835)	(.00402)	(.04415)	(.00986)	(.91147)	(.51590)	(.00000)
Income from Ferrous Metals	—	—	−872.68	—	—	—	−102.063	—	—	—	—	—
			(.00060)				(.03026)					
Rate of Profit, Mfg	—	—	—	—	—	—	—	—	—	—	—	—

	(1)	(2)	(3)	(4)	(5)	(6)	(7)	(8)	(9)	(10)	(11)	(12)
Dividend Income	—	—	—	—	—	-504.214 (.05373)	—	—	—	—	—	—
Mfg Unemp	—	—	-143.653 (.04888)	—	—	—	4,389.82 (.76501)	—	—	—	—	—
War Deaths	-8.00349 (.17002)	139.273 (.05547)	—	—	—	—	—	-91.879 (.03002)	—	—	—	.01127 (.00100)
CPD Activity[a]	5,763.78 (.77217)	461,480 (.15000)	539,257 (.12130)	449,304 (.00209)	627,265 (.30420)	36,444.5 (.94388)	165,846 (.17351)	1,481,660 (.04300)	585,853 (.00000)	1,217.9 (.14379)	3,718.9 (.02700)	401.68 (.00000)
Earnings Per Share	34,996.5 (.01006)	462,759 (.01360)	-335,459 (.04440)	152,878 (.00012)	—	—	115,310 (.00288)	140,538 (.46038)	105,025 (.00000)	—	166,061 (.00010)	59.160 (.00045)
Adj R²	.741	.738	.558	.779	.607	.522	.767	.812	.871	.844	.914	.861
Box-Pierce Q Stat.	11.04 (.0873)	12.15 (.0586)	11.097 (.0857)	9.42 (.1513)	6.87 (.3333)	2.49 (.8699)	8.41 (.2098)	9.49 (.1481)	12.42 (.0533)	7.96 (.2409)	4.82 (.5669)	4.07 (.5400)

#First pseudo-difference correction.

[a]Committee on the Present Danger Activity Lagged 2 years unless otherwise noted.

[b]Numbers in parenthesis are probability values for t-tests of the coefficients.

[c]A "—" indicates variable had no significant effect at P < .05 and the presence of the variable introduced problems with the regression estimate. For Communication and Total Procurement Expenditures, however, the lagged dependent variables were statistically discernible at P < .05 but introduced serious and uncorrectable problems with autocorrelation.

residuals. The presence or absence of these problem variables seemed to make no important changes in the other coefficients produced by the regressions. Consequently, the difficulties with these variables do not influence the interpretation of these data I present here.

As I expected, multicollinearity among the independent variables was a problem with some variables. The correlation between income from assets abroad and CPD activity is .86. Consequently, I present three tables in this analysis. Table 5.3 shows models including both CPD activity and income from assets abroad as well as the rest of the important variables. Table 5.5 excludes income from assets abroad. Table 5.7 includes income from assets abroad but excludes CPD activity. A comparison of the three tables shows no important differences in the magnitude and direction of the estimated coefficients for the other independent variables used here between models including CPD activity and income from assets abroad and models excluding either one of these two variables. I focus on table 5.3 for my discussion of the effects of defense contractor profitability, table 5.5 for my discussion of CPD activity, and table 5.7 for my discussion of income from assets abroad.

Table 5.3 shows that top defense contractor profits are not negatively related to any expenditure category as theory predicts. This gives little or no support for the hypothesized countercyclical interpretation of the effects of defense contractor political enterprise on defense resource allocation. Indeed, the effects of profits on procurement expenditures on ammunition, chemical, electrical and electronic equipment, armored vehicles, operations and maintenance, and total procurement expenditures are positive. Only the effect for weapons expenditures is in the expected direction. I could not estimate an autocorrelation free model for aircraft, ships, and RDT&E expenditures that contained the earnings variable. However, even with the high levels of detected autocorrelation in these models, the probabilities of the t-ratios for the earnings per share variable were very large (no model with significant autocorrelation is in any of the tables). The coefficients for guided missiles, electronic equipment, operations and maintenance, and total procurement are significant at levels well below the corrected alpha level of .0042. All other estimated coefficients are significant at $P \leq .05$. The clear trend in the effects of earnings per share on procurement expenditures (especially considering the highly significant effects for the aggregate measure of procurement) suggests that it is acceptable to relax the requirement for a Bonferoni correction for the chemicals and ammunition models.

Table 5.4 details the estimated coefficients for the profits variable and compares the magnitude of each coefficient with the maximum and mean of each corresponding procurement category. A change in one dollar in earnings per share increases the following year's expenditures $463 million for ammunition, $35 million for chemicals, $382 million for guided missiles, $90 million for armored vehicles, $110 million for electrical and electronic equipment, $1.6 billion for operations and maintenance, and $6.2 billion for total procurement. However, every dollar increase in earnings per share decreases weapons expenditures $337 million. As a percentage of both the mean and the maximum values of the dependent variables, these coefficient estimates are all relatively large. In all but one case, when profits go up, the following year's expenditures increase, when profits decline the following year's expenditures decline. These results warrant exploring an alternative explanation for the effects of defense industry political activities on defense contract allocation.

Table 5.5 indicates that the trend for CPD activity is more clear than that for earnings per share. CPD activity dramatically increases expenditures for all categories of expenditures except, as expected, ammunition and chemicals. The models with the least problems from autocorrelation and the best fit are with CPD activity lagged two years, although models with a lag of one year (not shown here) show very similar effects.[4] Estimating weapons expenditures with a model including CPD activity proved problematic. For every dependent variable except weapons, chemical, and ammunition expenditures the estimated coefficients are significantly smaller than the corrected P value of .0042.

Table 5.6 shows that with the exception of ammunition, chemical, and aircraft expenditures, maximum CPD activity resulted in very large increases in expenditures, in every case over $380 million. In the cases of ships, armored vehicles, communications equipment, and electronics the effects of CPD activity are especially large, from 58 percent of the mean for communications to an impressive 104 percent of the mean for armored vehicles. Maximum CPD activity

Table 5.4. Comparison of Regression Coefficients for Earnings per Share from Table 5.3

Variable	Maximum	Earnings Per Share Coefficient	Mean	% Mean	% Maximum
Ammunition	4,121,000	462,759	1,536,600	30	11
Chemicals	271,190	34,996.50	78,037	44	12
Weapons	707,200	-336,526	387,510	86	47
Missiles	4,353,000	382,169	2,622,800	14	8
Aircraft	8,639,000	0	4,949,200	0	0
Ships	3,218,000	0	1,644,000	0	0
Tanks	765,600	89,542.10	413,390	21	11
Comm.	5,168,000	333,664	2,657,500	12	6
Electronics	824,300	110,897	519,100	21	13
RDT&E ($1 Mills)	12,240	0	8,621	0	0
Operations & Maintenance ($1 Mills)	31,630	1,631.20	23,682	6	5
Total Procurement ($100 Mills)	1,005	61.57	779	7	6

has a weaker effect on guided missile expenditures. For the aggregated expenditure categories maximum CPD activity has a uniform positive effect boosting RDT&E expenditures just over a billion dollars, operations and maintenance expenditures about four billion dollars, and total procurement expenditures 11 billion dollars. These results are consistent with my expectations.

Not surprisingly, the estimated effects of income from assets abroad are very similar to those estimated for CPD activity. Table 5.7 indicates that income from assets abroad has statistically significant and positive effects on expenditures for guided missiles, ships, armored vehicles, RDT&E, operations and maintenance, and total procurement at $P \leq .0042$. The probability of the resulting t-ratio for expenditures on electronic equipment is .04753, well above the corrected alpha. Considering the obvious trend in the effects of this variable, I accept this coefficient as also being statistically important. The income from assets abroad variable does not have a statistically discernible influence on ammunition, chemicals, weapons, aircraft, and communications expenditures. The models estimating expenditures on ships and armored vehicles do not include the earning per share variable because of intractable autocorrelation.

Table 5.8 shows that income from assets abroad has the strongest influence on expenditures for ships, tanks, and electronics. Every $10 billion increase in income from assets abroad increments expenditures on ships $445.5 million, tanks about $193.33 million (47 percent of the mean, 25 percent of the maximum), and electronics expenditures nearly $66 million. The effect of income from assets abroad on weapons expenditures appears large with a $10 billion increase in income resulting in an increase in expenditures of $169.3 million (21 percent of the mean). However, the variation of the income variable around expenditures on weapons is so large that the t-ratio of the income coefficient is significant at $P \leq .15$. The effect of income from assets abroad on guided missile expenditures is weaker than for expenditures on ships, tanks, or electronics with every $10 billion in income increasing guided missile expenditures by only $79.5 million.

The influence income from assets abroad has on the three aggregate expenditure variables is consistently positive, but not as strong as for the procurement expenditure categories. Every increase in income of $10 billion boosts expenditures on RDT&E about $358

Table 5.5. OLS Regression Coefficients from Best Models Estimating Procurement Expenditures from Committee on the Present Danger Activity, Earnings per Share, and Economic Measures, Excluding Income from Assets Abroad with Corrections for Autocorrelation

Independent Variable	Chem.	Ammo.	Weapons	Guided Missiles	Aircraft	Ships	Armored Vehicles	Comm. DFR(1)#	Elect. Eqpt.	RDT&E	O&M	Total Proc.
Constant	-57,804	-137,562	4,938,640	-157,802	2,949,650	1,594,620	81,723.9	493,635	148,458	-371.198	-435.94	-124.4
	(.05470)[b]	(.77437)	(.00001)	(.04195)	(.00076)	(.00001)	(.64489)	(.19815)	(.01205)	(.64412)	(.8161)	(.2363)
Lagged Dept Variable	.891227	.163573	-.071957	.239415	.479141	-.003219	-.092696	.396115	-.02156	1.01745	.79545	.96830
	(.01016)	(.55439)	(.63697)	(.06747)	(.00153)	(.73537)	(.62549)	(.00590)	(.85067)	(.00000)	(.0000)	(.0000)
Inc. from Assets Abr.	N.A.[c]	N.A.	N.A.	N.A.	N.A.	N.A.	N.A.	N.A.	N.A.	N.A.	N.A.	N.A.
Inc. from Iron	—[d]	—	-917.141	—	—	—	-52.129	—	—	—	—	—
			(.00056)				(.31332)					
Rate of Profit, Mfg	—	67,413	—	36,924	145,164	-18,316	62,763	—	27.648	-8.972	3.987	—
		(.08799)		(.47619)	(.06518)	(.07408)	(.05413)		(.63912)	(.92694)	(.2586)	
Income from Dividends	—	—	—	—	—	—	12,913.3	—	—	—	—	—
							(.40106)					
Mfg Unemp.	—	—	-129,379	—	—	—	—	—	—	—	—	—
			(.05160)									

	(1)	(2)	(3)	(4)	(5)	(6)	(7)	(8)	(9)	(10)	(11)	(12)
War Deaths	-7.22649 (.17225)	40.023 (.05501)	—	—	—	—	—	-27.7769 (.34739)	—	—	—	-.0073 (.0854)
CPD Activity[a]	5,989 (.78114)	471,503 (.14703)	—	382,169 (.00004)	627.264 (.30420)	1,032,560 (.00455)	431,474 (.00106)	1,563,250 (.00069)	424,487 (.00000)	1,135.63 (.00157)	4,066.9 (.0000)	106.77 (.0002)
Earnings Per Share	34,996 (.01006)	463,593 (.01402)	-336,526 (.04420)	382,169 (.00009)	—	—	89,542.1 (.04295)	333,664 (.03600)	110,897 (.00010)	—	1,631.2 (.0008)	61.568 (.0000)
Adj R²	.71	.73	.56	.79	.61	.41	.63	.68	.49	.85	.91	.91
Box-Pierce Q Statistic	10.97 (.0894)	11.88 (.0572)	10.21 (.1159)	7.73 (.2590)	6.87 (.3333)	3.62 (.7282)	2.57 (.8603)	6.79 (.3045)	8.23 (.2219)	8.38 (.2113)	4.73 (.5787)	10.41 (.0643)

#First pseudo-difference correction.

[a]Committee on the Present Danger Activity Lagged 2 years unless otherwise noted.

[b]Numbers in parenthesis are probability values for t-tests of the coefficients.

[c]A "—" indicates variable had no significant effect at P < .05 and the presence of the variable introduced problems with the regression estimate. For Communication and Total Procurement Expenditures, however, the lagged dependent variables were statistically discernible at P < .05 but introduced serious and uncorrectable problems with autocorrelation.

[d]N.A. indicates the variables was not applicable to this table.

Table 5.6. Comparison of Regression Coefficients for the Committee on the Present Danger from Table 5.5.

Variable	Maximum	CPD Coefficient	Mean	% Mean	% Maximum
Ammunition	4,121,000	461,480	1,536,600	30	11
Chemicals	271,190	5,989.78	78,037	7	2
Weapons	707,200	0	387,510	0	0
Missiles	4,353,000	382,169	2,622,800	14	8
Aircraft	8,639,000	627,264	4,949,200	12	7
Ships	3,218,000	1,032,560	164.4000	62	32
Tanks	765,600	4.31,474	413,390	104	56
Comm.	5,168,000	1,563,250	2,657,500	58	30
Electronics	824,300	424,487	519,100	81	51
RDT&E ($1 Mills)	12,240	1,135.63	8,621	13	9
Operations & Maintenance ($1 Mills)	31,630	4,066.90	23,682	17	12
Total Procurement ($100 Mills)	1,005	106.78	779	13	10

million, operations and maintenance $1.1 billion, and total procurement $2.9 billion (4.15 percent, 4.65 percent, and 3.73 percent of the means, respectively).

The only measure of budgetary politics to appear in the final models is the lagged dependent variable. Many organizational researchers hypothesize that last year's budget represents the role of bureaucratic inertia in any government decision process. In my analysis the effect of this variable is most important for the aggregate expenditures. For expenditures on RDT&E, operations and maintenance, and total procurement the effects of last year's expenditures are statistically discernible at $P \leq .00000$. For each category a one unit change in last year's expenditures results in about a one unit change in this year's expenditures, an apparently strong relationship. For the individual categories of procurement, the effects of last year's expenditures are not so important. Last year's expenditures are significant at $P \leq .0042$ only for communications and aircraft expenditures. Depending on the model, last year's chemical expenditures are discernible at $P \leq .0051$ to $P \leq .012$. In table 5.7 last year's expenditures are significant at $P < .003$, but not in the other tables. These results give some support for this central aspect of the bureaucratic politics approach. But because of the complexities of interpreting coefficients from lagged dependent variables, the statistical results for last year's expenditures are not easily interpretable. These results could just be an artifact of certain types of autocorrelation or of variables not measured in the regression model (see Johnston 1984; Judge et al. 1980). Thus, the data, while somewhat consistent with a state politics model, could also simply be a statistical artifact of my choice of measures or the specific nature of my dependent variables.

Conclusion

The effects of CPD activity and income from assets abroad on the measures of expenditures are as expected. Both CPD activity and income from assets abroad have relatively strong and consistent effects on most categories of expenditures on hardware and unimportant effects on expenditures on supplies. That the effects for both

Table 5.7. OLS Regression Coefficients from Best Models Estimating Procurement Expenditures from Earnings per Share, and Economic Measures, Including Income from Assets Abroad with Corrections for Autocorrelation

Independent Variable	Chem.	Ammo.	Weapons	Guided Missiles	Aircraft	Ships	Armored Vehicles	Comm. DFR(1)#	Elect. Eqpt.	RDT&E	O&M	Total Proc.
Constant	-57,804 (.05470)[b]	-137,562 (.77437)	4,938,640 (.00001)	-157,802 (.04195)	2,949,650 (.00076)	1,594,620 (.00001)	81,723.9 (.64489)	493,635 (.19815)	148,458 (.01205)	-371.198 (.64412)	-435.94 (.8161)	-124.4 (.2363)
Lagged Dept Variable	.891227 (.01016)	.163573 (.55439)	-.071957 (.63697)	.239415 (.06747)	.479141 (.00153)	-.003219 (.73537)	-.092696 (.62549)	.396115 (.00590)	-.02156 (.85067)	1.01745 (.00000)	.79545 (.0000)	.96830 (.0000)
Inc. from Assets Abr.	N.A.[c]	N.A.	N.A.	—	N.A.	N.A.	N.A.	N.A.	N.A.	N.A.	N.A.	N.A.
Inc. from Iron	—[d]	—	-917.141 (.00056)	—	—	—	-52.129 (.31332)	—	—	—	—	—
Rate of Profit, Mfg	—	67,413 (.08799)	—	36,924 (.47619)	145,164 (.06518)	-18,316 (.07408)	62,763 (.05413)	—	27.648 (.63912)	-8.972 (.92694)	3.987 (.2586)	—
Income from Dividends	—	—	—	—	—	—	12,913.3 (.40106)	—	—	—	—	—
Mfg Unemp.	—	—	-129,379 (.05160)	—	—	—	—	—	—	—	—	—

	1	2	3	4	5	6	7	8	9	10	11	12
War Deaths	-7.22649 (.17225)	40.023 (.05501)	—	—	—	—	—	-27.7769 (.34739)	—	—	—	-.0073 (.0854)
CPD Activity[a]	5,989 (.78114)	471,503 (.14703)	—	382,169 (.00004)	627,264 (.30420)	1,032,560 (.00455)	431,474 (.00106)	1,563,250 (.00069)	424,487 (.00000)	1,135.63 (.00157)	4,066.9 (.0000)	106.77 (.0002)
Earnings Per Share	34,996 (.01006)	463,593 (.01402)	-336,526 (.04420)	382,169 (.00009)	—	—	89,542.1 (.04295)	333,664 (.03600)	110,897 (.00010)	—	1,631.2 (.0008)	61.568 (.0000)
Adj R^2	.71	.73	.56	.79	.61	.41	.63	.68	.49	.85	.91	.91
Box-Pierce Q Statistic	10.97 (.0894)	11.88 (.0572)	10.21 (.1159)	7.73 (.2590)	6.87 (.3333)	3.62 (.7282)	2.57 (.8603)	6.79 (.3045)	8.23 (.2219)	8.38 (.2113)	4.73 (.5787)	10.41 (.0643)

[a]Committee on the Present Danger Activity Lagged 2 years unless otherwise noted.

[b]Numbers in parenthesis are probability values for t-tests of the coefficients.

[c]A "—" indicates variable had no significant effect at $P < .05$ and the presence of the variable introduced problems with the regression estimate. For Communication and Total Procurement Expenditures, however, the lagged dependent variables were statistically discernible at $P < .05$ but introduced serious and uncorrectable problems with autocorrelation.

[d]N.A. indicates the variables was not applicable to this table.

Table 5.8. Comparison of Regression Coefficients for Income from Assets Abroad from Table 5.7

Variable	Maximum	Income from Assets Abroad*	Mean	% Mean	% Maximum
Ammunition	4,121,000	6,700	1,536,600	.44	.16
Chemicals	271,190	5,800	78,037	7.43	2.14
Weapons	707,200	169,300	387,510	20.51	11.24
Missiles	4,353,000	79,500	2,622,800	3.03	1.82
Aircraft	8,639,000	11,300	4,949,200	0.23	0.13
Ships	3,218,000	445,500	1,644,000	27.10	13.84
Tanks	765,600	193,330	413,390	46.77	25.25
Comm.	5,168,000	185,500	2,657,500	6.98	3.59
Electronics	824,300	64,500	519,100	12.43	7.82
RDT&E ($1 Mills)	12,240	358	8,621	4.15	2.92
Operations & Maint ($1 Mills)	31,630	1,100	23,682	4.65	3.48
Total Procurement ($100s Mills)	1,005	29	779	3.73	2.889

*Calculated in $10s of Billions.

of these variables are strongest for expenditures on ships, armored vehicles, guided missiles, and electronic and electrical equipment buttresses this conclusion.[5] These categories of weapons are necessary for effective force projection into the lesser developed world (for example, these weapons all played key roles in the destruction of Iraq's armed forces). Not only does the political action of the New Right increase aggregated expenditures on the military, but elite social movement political action and corporate income from assets abroad influence the allocation of weapons expenditures across categories of weapons. The data provides good support for the expected role of elite political activities and of economic interests abroad in the allocation of military expenditures.

The results presented here are inconsistent with two central approaches to explaining the allocation of military expenditures. First, the estimated effects of earnings per share are not consistent with my expectations. Rather than the proposed negative relationship between earnings per share and the various expenditure categories, a consistent positive relationship appears in the data. Falling profits among the top fifteen contractors, does not lead to increasing military expenditures as much current literature suggests, but instead to further decreases in military expenditures. This result counsels that researchers must explore an alternative explanation of the role defense contractor profits and political action play in defense resource allocation. More specifically, while defense contractor profits play an important role in the allocation of defense dollars, clearly the bailing out of defense firms in economic trouble is not, *on the average*, an important determinant of expenditures. Considering that defense firms are only rarely in dire financial straits (for example, one author found only seven aircraft firms experiencing significant financial trouble between 1946 and 1978 [Bright 1978 reported in Hooks 1990]), it is likely that bailouts do not occur often enough to show important effects in a time series analysis like this one.

The second unexpected outcome is the lack of any important effects of the macroeconomic variables suggested by the most common formulation of the monopoly capital model appearing in the data. With occasional exceptions (most often profit from ferrous metals with expenditures on weapons and armored vehicles) that do not appear to indicate any trend, no measure of the domestic economic performance of monopoly capital has any important effects on allocating military resources. This is contrary to Griffin et al.'s (1982a, 1982b) findings. However, I use data from a different period (1962–1986 compared to 1949–1977) as well as a different set of dependent variables. Hence, it is not unexpected that my results diverge from Griffin, Devine and Wallace's. It is important to realize, however, that the monopoly sector variables common to both my study and Griffin et al.'s—manufacturing sector unemployment and manufacturing rate of profit—were weak and unstable performers in their analyses. Still, the data presented do not provide even the weak support for this aspect of the monopoly capital approach that Griffin et al. found (Griffin, Devine, and Wallace 1982a; 1982b).

6

ASSESSING THE RESULTS

General Findings

A PRIMARY PURPOSE of this project is to compare the relative influence of forces exogenous to the state with forces endogenous to the state on policy outcomes. I refer you to the simplified path diagram of these forces as described in previous chapters shown in figure 1.3. In general the results support many of the relationships indicated in that diagram, but with some important modifications. Of special note is that only one factor endogenous to the state, bureaucratic inertia, appears to have any influence on military expenditures. This variable has a significant positive effect on chemical, aircraft, RDT&E, operations and maintenance, and total procurement expenditures. However, the difficulties in interpreting lagged dependent variables make these results open to several different interpretations. The other endogenous factors examined here, electoral politics, large-scale bureaucratic competition, and budgetary process, had no important effects on expenditures. In a general sense the data provide good support for the proposed relationships between the exogenous factors and military expenditure allocation. New Right social movement activity proved to be a powerful influence on military expenditures, greatly increasing many types of expenditures at the movement's peak. The effect of the value of corporate interests abroad was also as hypothesized. However, the data did not reflect the proposed relationship between defense contractor profits and expenditures, that low profits would lead to higher expenditures. Instead, the data indicated that higher profits lead to more expenditures. Finally, these disparities between the nature of my initially hypothesized relationships and the observed relationships as well as the limits on the data suggest a number of paths that future research using similar data should take.

The Military-Industrial Complex Approach

The preponderance of the extant literature on the political economy of military procurement suggests that the state provides counter-cyclical infusions of income to defense contractors through defense contracts. The mechanisms linking the profit requirements of defense contractors with the decision process are the political action of defense firms and the policy biases built into the contract award system since the turn of the century. The data I present here, how-ever, do not support the central contention of this approach. My analysis indicates that when it comes to defense expenditures, it is successful accumulation, rather than a failure to accumulate, that opens the coffers of the state to exploitation by capital. Except to say that compared with non-defense firms, few defense firms face hard economic times, the existing literature examining defense contractor profits and political behavior sheds little light on the source of this counter-theoretical finding. Consequently, bailouts must be too in-frequent to influence the statistical results of my analysis. There is nothing obvious about the pattern of relationships between earnings per share and the various measures of military expenditures that points to a non-speculative explanation.

One possible explanation of the findings on defense contractor profits is the use of a measure of *total* firm profits. Perhaps only managers in charge of the parts of the firms that are involved in defense contracting direct the political activity of the firm. This could mean that the profits of these subsidiaries or branches of the defense firm might be a more direct indicator of the forces spurring political action. However, many of the examples of government bail-outs of defense contractors, for example, Chrysler and Lockheed, came about because of problems with the civilian side of these firms' business. Also, many of the top fifteen contractors such as General Dynamics, Grumman, Rockwell International, and Hughes Corporation do only a limited amount of non-defense business. The consistency and strength of the observed relationships between earnings per share and the various categories of defense procurement expenditures suggest that these results are unlikely to be simply spurious statistical artifacts.

Alternatively, I suggest that it is the level of material interests that determines the amount of a firm's political action rather than whether the firm is profitable. The approach outlined in chapter 2 hypothesized that declining profitability would lead a firm to undertake more political action to enhance its profit outlook. The data analysis, however, indicates that higher profits produce higher expenditures the following year. These results and recent research on the determinants of business political action suggest the alternative model shown in figure 6.1.

In this model, increasing profits are the outgrowth of increasing contract awards and the firm's political action is the result of its contract awards rather than being from the firm's profitability. This political action then maintains or increases future contract awards. Defense contractor political behavior is linked not to declining profits, but to the value to the firm of the defense contracts.[1] It is likely that both profits and firm political action covary with last year's profits and political action. In this model, profit is not the causal force behind either contract awards or firm political action, instead it is the existing level of firm material connections to the state in the form of contract awards that influences firm political behavior. Perhaps one component of the observed relationship between last year's military expenditures and this year's expenditures is the feedback mechanism I propose here between last year's contract awards through a firm's political action to this year's contract awards. What I suggest here is a more detailed version of the political mechanisms making up the follow-on imperative described by Kurth (1978). Indeed, these findings appear to support this aspect of the politic economy surrounding military contract allocation.

Good evidence exists in other literatures on large business political behavior that is very supportive of this alternative interpretation

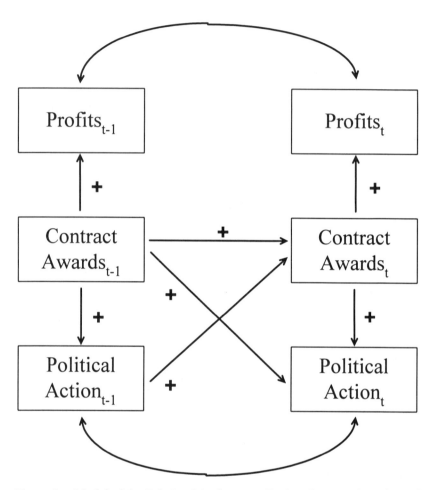

Figure 6.1. Model of the Relationships between Profits, Contract Awards, and Defense Contractor Profits

of defense contract politics. Research on political action committees (PACs) indicates that the value to the firm of the relationship it has with the state, for example, the amount of defense contracts, the quantity of mergers and acquisitions, and the number of legal actions the state has taken against the firm, largely determines the size of business-sponsored political action committees (Boies 1989). Each of these types of interrelations the firm has with the state entails a great deal of haggling with state bureaucracies, haggling that can be made easier and less regular if the firm can gain assistance from friendly bureaucrats or members of Congress. The profitability of the firm, however, has no important influence on a firm's PAC receipts. Other researchers have also noted relationships between firm material interest and political action (for example, Etzioni 1984; Gais 1983; Pittman 1977). A firm's political behavior appears to be dependent on the material interest ties the firm has with the state, regardless of the profitability of those ties.

The Committee on the Present Danger and Foreign Investment Interests

The CPD is a core social movement organization of the New Right social movement. The activities of the CPD and, consequently, a significant aspect of the New Right, is highly correlated with the amount of corporate income from U.S.-owned assets abroad (CPD activity and Income from assets abroad are correlated at $R = .86$). The magnitude of this correlation suggests that it is more than coincidence. Figure 6.2 illustrates very dramatically the covariation between these two variables and their relationship to total procurement. The data I present here support my initial expectation that the activities of the CPD would positively influence military expenditures. The strong relationship between the behavior of the CPD and the income variable, however, indicates that a more complex explanation linking the behavior of the CPD to the large scale structural processes posited by Baran and Sweezy (1966) may be in order. I initially posited that the organization of the CPD was an outgrowth of elite reaction to President Carter's adoption of a less belligerent and more cooperative foreign policy toward the Soviet Union and other, less developed nations, and of the rise of the New Right in the United States toward the end of the 1970s. I did not, however, posit a primary cause of elite interest in organizing against Jimmy Carter's foreign and military policies or of the formation of

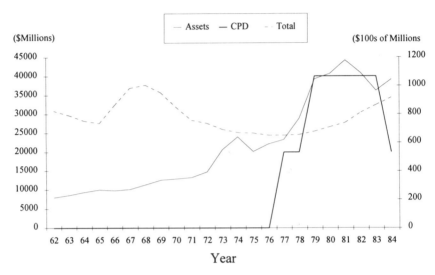

Figure 6.2. Total Procurement, Income from Assets Abroad, and CPD Activity by Year

the New Right. The high correlation between the activities of the CPD and corporate income from overseas assets suggests that a material basis exists for the formation of the CPD as well as the more general New Right movement.

Along with having many people on the board of directors who are linked with New Right political organizations, many members of the CPD board are linked with investment capital. Table 3.5 shows that of the 110 businesses with some form of tie to the CPD board of directors, the plurality of firms (39 percent) are financial firms of some type. Heavily represented in this group are investment firms such as Dillon, Reed, and Company and Goldman, Sachs, and Company[2] and banks with significant investments overseas such as Citibank. The second most common type of firms (34 percent) are big multinational industrial firms such as Temple-Eastex, Ingersoll-Rand, Honeywell, and Hewlett-Packard. For many firms, Hewlett-Packard and Goldman, Sachs, and Company, for example, high-level executives of the firm are also the CPD board of directors. Not only is there a statistical relationship between the CPD and overseas material interests, but a number of important organizations and individuals directly connected to these overseas interests are among the founders of this political organization.

I believe the evidence is strong that the activities of the New Right through the CPD, income from assets abroad, and specific types of military expenditures are somehow related. That the strongest relationships I find in these data between CPD activity or income from assets abroad and the measures of military expenditures are for such expenditure categories as operations and maintenance, ships, armored vehicles, and guided missiles indicates the existence of a real link between the value of overseas investment and military policy. Many scholars see these types of expenditures as largely being related to force projection in lesser developed nations, either to purchase weapons suitable for force projection or to actually carry out operations (Forsberg 1986). An excellent case in point is the role played by our sophisticated armor, electronics, and naval weapons (especially carrier-based aircraft and ship-based Tomahawk cruise missiles) in the recent Gulf War.

The data I have presented so far in this book, however, do not clarify the nature of the relationship among the overseas interest variable, CPD behavior, and military expenditures. In figures 6.3, 6.4, and 6.5, I propose three alternative ways these variables might be related. In figure 6.3 I propose that the value of investments abroad directly affects both CPD activity and the procurement of interventionist weapons. CPD activity also directly affects procurement. Traditional monopoly capital theory posits that the state acts, at least in part, as a manager of the interests of big capital. Consequently, capitalists and their agents directly organize to lobby government, and state managers recognize the necessity of the state to protect the foreign interests of U.S.-based firms. Because many individuals on the CPD board of directors became members of the state management cadre when Reagan was elected, the concerns of the CPD became the concerns of the state managers by 1981. This virtually guaranteed that the state would act to increase protection of these overseas assets.

The path diagram in figure 6.4 indicates a possibly larger role for the CPD. I believe it is reasonable, considering Gold's work on the initial formation of the early Cold War "Keynesian Coalition"

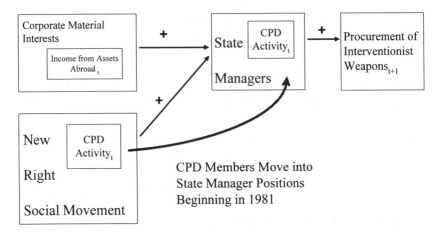

Figure 6.3. Model with Elite Social Movement Activity and Overseas Investment Directly Influencing Procurement

(1977:143), to posit that the CPD was the mechanism that transmitted the desire of multinational capital to protect its increasingly valuable overseas investments by expanding military expenditures of certain types to the federal government. Gold's work indicated that the coalition of forces that produced the cold war and military Keynesianism was mainly " . . . New Deal social spending advocates dedicated to Keynesian style intervention, Cold War protagonists

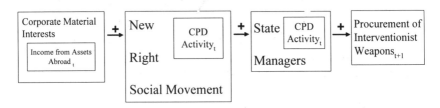

Figure 6.4. Model with Elite Social Movement Activity Intervening between Interests and Procurement

interested in the containment of the Soviet Union, and elite business people committed to the expansion of monopoly capital" (Griffin, Devine, and Wallace 1982a:S116). The members of the founding board of directors of the Committee on the Present Danger (see Appendix B) represent many of the same groups and organizations that Gold concludes supported post–World War II military Keynesianism. Archenemies of the Soviet Union such as Richard Pipes, noted liberals such as Bayard Rustin, and many elite businessmen such as David Packard, John B. Connally, and John T. Connor (president of Allied Chemical) as well as many labor leaders were all members of the CPD founding board of directors. The list of the founding board of directors of the first Committee on the Present Danger organized in December of 1950 provided by Sanders (1983:87) indicates that the founders of the first CPD were remarkably similar to those of the second. The CPD and the New Right movement might prove to be the central mechanisms through which the profit requirements of big capital are transmitted to the central government (see Edsall 1984; Ferguson and Rogers 1981). In this model structural forces are important because they induce political action by members of the upper class who are affected by the changes in the economic structure. It is this political behavior that changes the course of state behavior. In this model the state has no significant autonomy from outside actors, particularly from organized members of the upper class. It is important to note that in this model the state is the instrument only of organized upper class political action, not of the upper class as a whole or of individual members of the upper class.

The last figure in this series, figure 6.5, proposes an entirely structural argument. Consistent with traditional Marxist-structuralist approaches that posit the state as the manager of the capitalist economy, the state responds to the increasing value of foreign investment by adopting policies to protect those increasingly valuable assets. In this example, the state's response was to increase expenditures on certain parts of the military. These changes in foreign income, in part, spurred the CPD into action. The increasing business activity overseas, or the increase in its contribution to capitalist accumulation, may have increased the interest of many people connected with that activity as well as perhaps making the scaling back of the military by

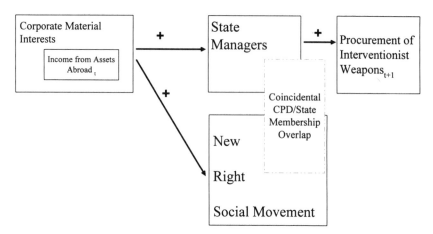

Figure 6.5. Model with Elite Social Movement Activity Only Resulting from Structural Forces

Jimmy Carter seem dangerous to many. But, it is the recognition by state managers that something must be done (or not done) that makes changes in policy occur, not political organizing by elites. Some additional evidence for this lies in the fact that a number of weapons systems purchased during the Reagan arms buildup were initiated by the Carter administration. These include the M-1 tank, Stealth bomber, and the air-launched and ground-launched cruise missiles. Indeed, the last two budgets of the Carter administration called for significant increases in procurement expenditures.

Furthermore, the increased amount of political action by many groups focused on the U.S. federal government during the 1970s and 1980s (for example, the number of registered lobbying organizations in Washington, D.C. increased to nearly twenty thousand by the early 1980s) may mean that the CPD was just one competing interest among many. Fred Block's (1977b) contention that the upper class in the United States is so competitive and disorganized that it cannot exert much influence on the state is consistent with this posited role for the CPD in defense policy formation. Thus the observed relationship between CPD activity and military outlays may simply be coincidental. However, that many members of the CPD as well as other

New Right political organizations became part of state management cadre once Reagan was elected is strong evidence that the state managers are not autonomous from society.

To examine the viability of these three alternative hypotheses I estimated a number of regression models with CPD activity as the dependent variable.[3] I examined the effects of all the independent variables listed in table 5.2 on CPD activity. None of these variables, however, had statistically important effects on CPD activity, even when lagged as much as three years with the exception of the gross rate of profit for the manufacturing sector lagged one year and corporate income from assets abroad, unlagged. I also examined the data for the presence of an interaction between the foreign income measure and CPD activity in models predicting procurement. The presence of an interaction would give support to the model described in figure 6.4 with the CPD intervening between the income variable and procurement. However, the data provide no evidence of any interaction between CPD activity and the foreign income measure for any of the procurement variables. The foreign income and rate of profit variables, while having statistically significant effects, produced models with significant autocorrelation. Moreover, significant collinearity between the two variables made it very problematic to make an interpretable model containing both variables. The autocorrelation also proved to be intractable. This suggests that model misspecification, possibly resulting from an unmeasured variable, might be a likely cause of the autocorrelation. This suggests that additional analysis of some economic factor related to U.S. foreign trade could prove fruitful in explaining the formation of the CPD. For several reasons oil prices and production are good candidates for additional investigation.

The role of oil in the U.S. and international economies is very significant. By 1985, 20 percent of the value of total international trade in goods was petroleum or petroleum products (Mikdashi 1986). Moreover, this trade has expanded both in value—due to the large price increases of 1973–1974 and 1979–1980—and in volume, especially during 1968–1979 when world oil production increased over 50 percent from fourteen billion barrels per year in 1968 to nearly twenty-three billion barrels in 1979 (Degolyer and Mac-Naughton 1989). Despite decreasing production of oil during the early 1980s, price increases caused large increases in the dollar value of the world oil trade until the mid-1980s when oil prices softened (Degolyer and MacNaughton 1989). Middle Eastern oil, especially oil from Kuwait, Iraq, Iran, and Saudi Arabia, has become the major component of the oil traded in international markets. Moreover, a small handful of corporations control the distribution of the vast majority of Middle Eastern oil. These companies are Mobil Oil, Exxon, Amoco, Chevron (which acquired Gulf Oil in 1984), and Texaco from the United States; British Petroleum from Great Britain; and Shell Oil from the Netherlands (Blair 1976; Mikdashi 1986).

The international oil trade also plays a key role in the international financial community. Increasing Middle Eastern oil exports have had very significant effects on exchange rates, especially the U.S. dollar's relationship to other Organization of Economic Cooperation and Development (OECD) currencies, as well as balance of payments (Mikdashi 1986). Moreover, the high value of Middle Eastern oil has directly and indirectly increased non–oil-exporting developing nations' foreign debts by as much as $260 billion between 1973 and 1982. International Monetary Fund (IMF) and U.S., European, and Japanese banks largely financed this debt (Cline 1983). Finally, the major oil companies, the "Seven Sisters" (now the six sisters), despite the huge cash flow from Middle Eastern oil (or more likely because of it), increased the amount of money they borrowed from banks. In the period from 1971 to 1982, borrowing by twenty-four major oil companies increased 2.75 times. Much of this debt financed acquisitions of other oil companies such as Chevron's 1984 $13.3 billion takeover of Gulf Oil (Mikdashi 1986). The price of Middle Eastern oil has now become a central factor in determining worldwide prices for oil (Fried and Blandin 1988). During the late 1970s and early 1980s the booming oil business spurred huge quantities of borrowing throughout the world to finance what turned out to be risky oil exploration and drilling (Mikdashi 1986).[4] The impact of the oil trade on financial markets has been considerable. Because nearly 40 percent of the companies with management or director connections to the founding board of directors of the CPD are some form of financial firm, it seems reasonable that the world oil trade might be of considerable interest to these firms and their management.

A last notable point of relevance about Middle Eastern oil is its effect on the world arms trade. The growth in production and increase in the price of oil during the 1970s and into the 1980s gave Middle Eastern nations huge increases in wealth. Paid for by these large cash surpluses, spurred on by the many extant conflicts in the area, and fertilized by East-West competition and conflict, a regional arms race ensued. In 1980 the Middle East accounted for 6.9 percent of total world expenditures on arms and 33.1 percent of world arms imports, the highest share for any region. Arms imports to the area grew at a rate of 14.77 percent annually from 1971 to 1980, more than tripling in real dollars (U.S. ACDA 1983). The United States supplied between one-quarter and one-half, depending on the type of weapon, of arms from all sources imported to this area from 1976 to 1980. For the period from 1977 to 1987 the Middle East has been the world's primary market for arms and military equipment.[5]

The constellation of concerns and interests just outlined, as well as more general concerns about adequate and relatively affordable energy supplies and their security, indicates that Middle Eastern oil production is a very central element to world trade and U.S. economic interests. More specifically, U.S. firms control much of the region's oil production, as well as much of the world oil trade, thus making the value of oil exported from the Middle East a central component of the value of U.S. corporate assets abroad. Thus, oil production and oil costs associated with the Middle East are closely linked to several central aspects of contemporary capitalism. The economic and political upheavals triggered by events in the Middle East oil fields challenged the legitimacy of the capitalist governments of the U.S. and Western Europe. Sharply increasing and later sharply falling oil prices reduced the rate of profit in many sectors of the capitalist economy. Furthermore, some sectors of the capitalist economy made tremendous profits because of rising oil prices. The primary cause of these price increases was the rising price of Middle Eastern oil. The price of Middle Eastern oil and the dependence of national economies on Middle Eastern oil are central to both crises of legitimacy and of profit and are key features of the value of overseas assets to large U.S. business.

I tap these three dimensions of the role of Middle Eastern oil in the U.S. economy with the price of Saudi Arabian crude oil in U.S.

dollars multiplied by the amount of crude oil exported from the Middle East in thousands of barrels for each year from 1962 to 1986; this gives a good estimate of the financial impact Middle Eastern oil production has on the rest of the world (from Degolyer and Mac-Naughton 1989). Also included in the analysis is the gross rate of profit for the manufacturing sector lagged one year and corporate income from assets abroad, unlagged, on the chance that the autocorrelation noted earlier was due to model misspecification.

The best OLS model predicting activity of the Committee on the Present Danger includes only the value of Middle Eastern oil variable and appears to be free of autocorrelation. The Durban-Watson statistic for this model of 1.33 falls between the 5 percent lower limit of 1.27 and upper limit of 1.66, thus this test for autocorrelation is inconclusive. However, the Box-Pierce Q statistic is only 7.00 and is significant at a $P = .3208$. The model fits fairly well, even considering the exaggerating effects of time series data, with an adjusted R^2 of .78. None of the other two variables tested here performed well in predicting CPD activity. Regardless of the lag or transformation neither variable had a t-ratio significant at $P \leq .10$. But, all three variables are highly collinear with Rs of .80 and greater, making a clear interpretation of the results difficult. The regression coefficient for the total value of Middle Eastern oil production is .5178 raised to the -5th power (a seemingly small number, but the value of oil production has a mean of 71,629, yielding a predicted value for CPD activity of 0.371 at the mean value of Middle Eastern oil production, somewhat above .29, the observed mean of CPD activity, see table 5.2), significant at $P \leq .00000$. This relationship is very apparent in figure 6.6, a time plot of CPD activity and value of Middle Eastern oil production by year. When the income from assets abroad and corporate profits measures are in the model the P for the Middle Eastern oil variable is only .02563.

These results, in conjunction with the results from the analysis of the military procurement data, indicate that important modifications must be made to my hypothesizing on the relationship between economic forces, elite political activity, and state policy. It appears that the relationship posited in figure 6.4 between income from assets abroad and CPD activity is not supported by the data. However, the CPD in particular and the New Right in general is clearly connected

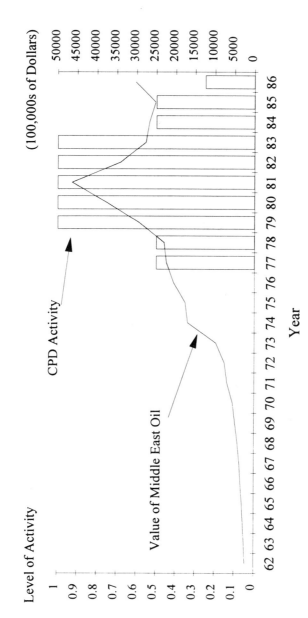

Figure 6.6. CPD Activity, Value of Middle Eastern Oil Production by Year

to important economic transformation and crises in the capitalist economy. A second economic change variable, the value of Middle Eastern oil, seems to be an important factor in the formation and dissolution of the CPD and possibly the larger New Right movement. The data suggest this modified model shown in figure 6.7.

It is, however, undeniable that the capitalist crises measure (gross manufacturing profits), the value of overseas investments measure (income from assets abroad), and the value of Middle Eastern oil, a variable measuring both an aspect of capitalist crisis as well as an aspect of overseas investment, are all interrelated. Another step in analysis is necessary to ferret out the actual structure of relationships among these variables. Moving to that next step in the analysis is for a later stage in this research.

Military procurement in the United States is not only directly influenced by the economic needs of multinational capital but also indirectly influenced by major economic crises. Considering the long-term institutionalized commitment of our foreign policy apparatus to protecting and promoting the interests of U.S.-owned capital abroad, the former conclusion is not unreasonable (Roy 1981; 1977). The latter effect, however, rather than being through long institutionalized channels in the executive branch's bureaucracy is instead through the domestic social movement organizing of very wealthy members of our society. These factors most strongly affect areas of military procurement that relate to foreign intervention. Thus, changes in the economy and polity do not only raise or lower the overall quantity of military hardware purchased by the U.S. military as most extant theory posits, but also change the kinds of things the U.S. military ultimately purchases. Contemporary research on the New Deal (Jenkins and Brents 1989; Quadagno 1984), steel policy in the United States since World War II (Prechel 1991; 1990), and tax reform, labor reform, and consumer protection legislation (Akard 1992) also concludes that successful business political unity and organization is spurred by capitalist crises. Note that the political activities I discuss related to defense contractor profits are related to the political behavior of individual firms, activities that can best be described as political entrepreneurship. The forces that spur the organization of individual firms (and individual capitalists) into larger

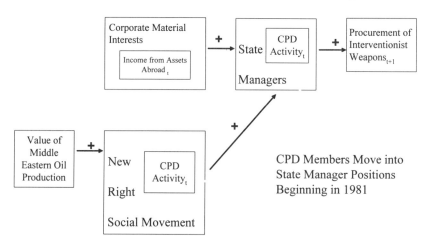

Figure 6.7. Modified Model with Elite Social Movement Activity and Overseas Investment Directly Influencing Procurement with Middle Eastern Oil Production Influencing Elite Social Movement Activity.

scale class-wide political organization are not the particularistic interests and risks individual firms encounter in day-to-day business, but instead are the infrequent crises that threaten the interests of large groups of firms and the interests of the owners of those firms. The activity of the CPD stems from class-wide crisis, but the activity of individual defense contractors stems from their particularistic relationship to the state.

Factors Endogenous to the State

The only force endogenous to the state that significantly influences the measures of military expenditures used in this study is bureaucratic inertia. The other endogenous factors examined here, electoral politics, large-scale bureaucratic competition, and budgetary process, did not prove to be statistically important. Many decisionmaking studies of budgets and of the military give great weight to bureaucratic inertia as a force in defense policy outcomes (Kennedy 1983; Fallows 1981; Gansler 1981; Wildavsky 1979; Gabriel and Savage 1978; Kaldor 1975; Armocost 1969). However, the measure of bureaucratic inertia, last year's budget, is not significant for nearly all the disaggregated measures of expenditures, but is highly significant for most of the aggregated measures. Additionally, autocorrelation plagued OLS regressions not reported here that contained the other independent variables shown in Tables 5.3, 5.5, and 5.7, but did not include a lagged dependent variable. In most instances Newey and West's counterpart to the "White estimator," a procedure to correct for first order autocorrelation, corrected this autocorrelation (Newey and West 1987; Greene 1989:181). Once last year's budget was included in the models, however, they became much better behaved and only a few had problems with autocorrelation.[6] Consequently, it is not unreasonable to conclude that other phenomena are entangled with the effects of last year's budget.

The observed relationships between last year's budget and the various measures of expenditures, at least in these data, might either be compensating for autocorrelation or measuring variables not included in the analysis as Johnston (1984) and Judge et al. (1980) suggest is often the case in time series analysis. The effect of last year's budget on the presence of autocorrelation lends credence to the former explanation.[7] The question of exactly what phenomena a lagged dependent variable is tapping is a problem ubiquitous to time series analysis that this book is unable to resolve. The data here, however, appear to suggest that bureaucratic inertia plays at least some role in the allocation of military resources. The research does not describe precisely how much of a role this variable plays in the allocation of military resources. Considering that the budgetary politics and, most especially, the state-centered approaches both place great theoretical importance on the influence of the endogenous factors that did not prove to be significant as well as budgetary inertia as primary determinants of state policy outcomes, the failure of these variables to have strong and clear cut effects indicates that this body of theory does not contribute a great deal to our understanding of what determines military expenditures.

Future Research on Disaggregated Military Expenditure Data

Perhaps the most important suggestion for improving future research using these data is to gather additional years of data on the
key dependent and independent variables. The data used here on
disaggregated military expenditures is only for 1962 through 1986.
Obviously, it will not be hard to add more recent data to these series
since the publications containing the data are currently readily available. However, simply adding more recent data is not enough to
significantly improve the generalizability of the results. During the
years before 1964, especially the early 1950s, many of the contemporary institutional arrangements relevant to the military were still
forming or were in fact different from their current form. Lobbying
techniques common among defense contractors are much more sophisticated today but also competition with other special interests is
more intense. Weapons technologies, methods of manufacture, as
well as a host of economic forces are considerably different. While in
many important respects the data set used here covers years with
many similarities to the nineteen years between the end of World
War II and 1964, there are important differences. Finally, some phenomena occurred in both the periods covered by these data and
before, most notably a huge peacetime arms buildup, a huge increase
in overseas material interests, and an elite social movement (the first
CPD). Finding comparable results from both time periods would
lend a great deal of support to my arguments concerning the role of
material interests in foreign policy decisionmaking.

Very importantly, almost all other researchers using quantitative
time series data begin their series in the mid-1950s or earlier. The data
I present here, therefore, is not wholly comparable in this important
respect to most other research. Comparing the results from this research with previous research is therefore more difficult. However,
my extensive searches for the government publications that contain
these data beginning in 1951 have been unsuccessful. If available,
this additional data would not only allow easier comparisons between this research and the research of other scholars, but it would
allow the testing of more variables at one time in the models. Addi-

tionally, a time series including data from 1951 to 1990 or 1991 would allow me to address the very significant problem presented recently by Isaac and Griffin (1989). These authors suggest that much time series analysis ends up treating many processes that change over time as a single "ahistorical" process. That is, any detectable relationship in the data is treated as existing over the entire time of the series. Its effects are averaged across the entire time series. They recommend a "temporally moving covariance" approach to overcoming this problem. A cruder way of testing for the same type of phenomenon is to be able to analyze a time series in smaller, substantively important groups of years. With only twenty-four years of data, neither approach is feasible.

Conclusion

The data I present here provide some important insight both into the functioning of the state and into why we buy the kinds of weapons we do. The data give good support to the contention that factors exogenous to the state are the more consistent and powerful forces at work shaping policy outcomes. The activities of the CPD and the more general New Right movement appear to have had a strong influence on arms expenditures in the United States. Large-scale capitalist crises and specific material interests are key components of understanding this particular process, perhaps causing both the formation of elite social movements as well as directly affecting the decisions of state managers (especially once the social movement members become active members of the state management cadre). Additionally the role of defense contractors in boosting military expenditures is clearly important. The exact role of defense contractor profits in the decision process, however, is still cloudy. Kurth's follow-on imperative is undoubtedly central to understanding the processes linking defense contractor profits, their political activities, and the allocation of procurement contracts. Broadly, I would now propose a simpler model of the key forces influencing military expenditures. Figure 6.8 indicates the general model for use in the next stage of research using disaggregated military expenditure data.

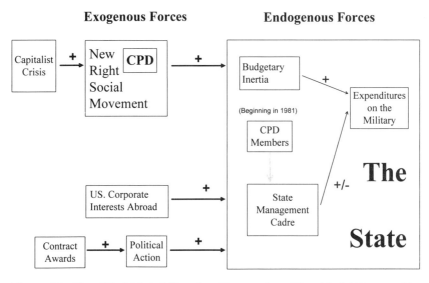

Figure 6.8. Simplified Model Showing Changes from First Model Proposed in Chapter 1

The most important changes in the model are the elimination of all but bureaucratic inertia from the list of forces endogenous to the state, the reversal of the sign for defense contractor profits from a negative to a positive, and the addition of capitalist crises (defined here as the value of Middle Eastern oil) as a cause of elite social movement behavior.

The key factors that appear to affect the types of military expenditures examined in this study are overseas material interests, elite social movement organization, and defense contractor profits, possibly through the follow-on imperative. Of less importance to expenditures, is bureaucratic inertia, although in the case of expenditures for RDT&E this variable has a powerful effect. It is very important to note that these major forces have differential effects on the different categories of military expenditures. The clearest pattern is that changes in the key exogenous factors, CPD activity and the value of overseas assets most strongly influence expenditures on ships, armored vehicles, communications, and the general category of operations and maintenance. That these categories of expenditures are among the most important types of expenditures for force projection in lesser developed nations indicates the remarkable responsiveness of the state to the political action and the needs of capitalists and their organizations in the U.S.

A clear example of the potential policy impact of the forces described in this book is the Rapid Deployment Force. Since the early 1960s there has been a significant interest in developing such a force by uniformed members of the state. Instead of spending money on such a force, the state reduced expenditures on one of the most important components of this kind of force, transport ships (Collins 1978). The late 1970s and early 1980s, however, saw large increments in expenditures on this component of the force, and an even larger investment in the purchasing and prepositioning of supplies overseas. The forward base most important to current defense goals is the recently enhanced facilities on the island of Diego Garcia in the Indian Ocean. The 1991 Persian Gulf War would have been very difficult to prosecute without this major change in policy.[8] A change in policy that is coincident with the actions of the New Right, the tremendous rise in U.S. corporate income from assets abroad, and, indirectly, the increasing role of Middle Eastern oil production in a key U.S.-dominated sector of the international economy. Indeed, a hint at the source of the recent Gulf War is that the value of Middle Eastern oil production is a major force influencing domestic political arrangements and later U.S. military capabilities.

The data provides good support for Baran and Sweezy's (1966) contention that a considerable part of U.S. military expenditures is the result of U.S. overseas interests. This data suggests that forces exogenous to the state are the most important factors determining major change in military procurement. This research indicates that major economic changes directly influence state policy as well as contribute to the formation of elite social movement organizations that affect national policy. The material interests of defense contractors also play a significant role in procurement decisions. These results indicate that, despite the end of the Cold War, significant reductions in arms spending by the United States will likely be very difficult to realize unless there are also significant reductions in the relative amount of income that U.S.-based corporations derive from their overseas investments and if a concerted political attack is waged against the political and bureaucratic processes linking defense profitability to expenditures. Indeed, the primary defense cuts initiated by both the Bush and Clinton administrations are disproportionately targeted towards the reduction of personnel and bases rather than the reductions of procurement expenditures.

The evidence in this book shows that forces outside the state significantly influence what is supposedly the most autonomous of U.S. central bureaucracies, the military. The state is not autonomous from the rest of society, especially from the wealthiest members of our society. A primary criticism of research proposing a significant role for the upper class in the formation of public policy is that it has failed to "demonstrate convincingly" that significant sectors or groups of capitalists play an important role in policymaking (Weir, Orloff, Skocpol 1988:14).[9] In contrast to this assertion, the research presented here provides evidence of just such a group in the form of the New Right Social Movement and the Committee on the Present Danger.

Another significant criticism leveled against the "corporate liberalism" perspective[10] by state-centric scholars is that " . . . it cannot specify the conditions under that interventions by dominant corporate interests will occur" (Block 1977b, cited in Quadagno 1984:632). The relationships between capitalist crises and the activity of the CPD and between CPD behavior and U.S. corporate interests abroad indicate that under conditions of major crisis or when capitalist investments become vulnerable, some segments of the capitalist class organize and intervene in the processes of state policy formation. Indeed, the data I present here and the work of Shoup (1980) and Sanders (1983) suggest that when capitalists conclude that the policy trajectory of the state is not meeting their profit accumulation needs, then politically *organized* capitalists make significant attempts to change the behavior of the state. The presence of accumulation crisis may also be a necessary condition for this high level of capitalist organization and cooperation (Useem 1983; Vogel 1989:290; Prechel 1990).

Finally, because many of the people active in the CPD before Reagan's election in 1980 went on to become high-level state managers under the Reagan administration, the separation between the state and civil society presented in much of the literature arguing for a state autonomous from civil society is not empirically accurate. The permeability of the state bureaucracies indicated by the movement of people between the military services and defense contractors (and vice versa) combined with the significant role business-dominated advisory councils play in policymaking provides additional support to this conclusion. The research presented here demonstrates that the state and the elite members of civil society in the United States are very closely intertwined.

In summary, this study demonstrates that state-society boundaries are permeable. This bolsters Poulantzas's (1978; see also Prechel 1991) argument that the state in capitalist society is a part of the mode of production. The findings of this research and of previous research, especially on the activities of the CPD and related organizations, suggest that class-segments both inside and outside the state significantly affect the behavior of the state. This supports a model of the state that is closer to the models presented in research and theory of scholars proposing a state more linked to class conflict and class politics (Baran and Sweezy 1966; Prechel 1990, 1991; Gilbert and Howe 1991; Domhoff 1990; Jenkins and Brents 1989; Quadagno 1984, 1987; and Poulantzas 1978, 1980) than to the models proposing a more autonomous state (Hooks 1990a, 1990b; Block 1977a, 1977b, 1987; Wildavsky 1979; Skocpol 1980) or the models of the pure structuralists such as Offe and Ronge (1982). The overall commitment of resources to the military as well as the distribution of resources within the various activities of the military in the United States is significantly influenced by social and political processes originating outside the state apparatus. However, the U.S. state and more specifically the U.S. military, are so deeply embedded in society and economy that neither has a truly independent existence.

APPENDIX A

Time Plots of the Dependent Variables

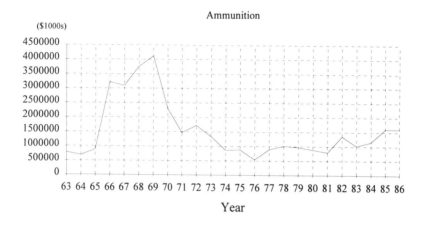

Ammunition

($1000s)

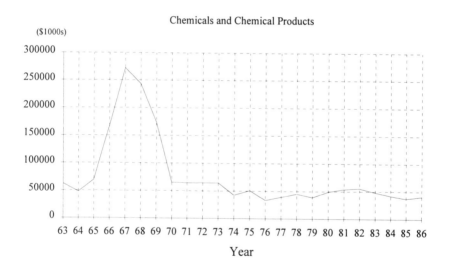

Chemicals and Chemical Products

($1000s)

146

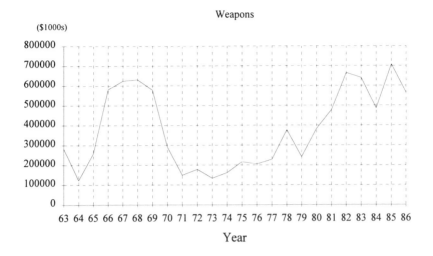

Weapons

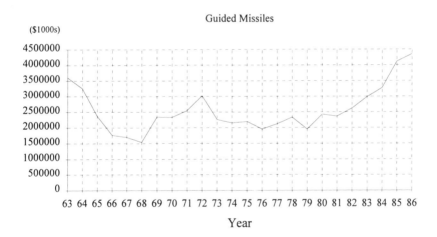

Guided Missiles

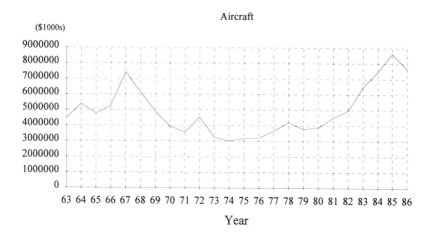

Aircraft

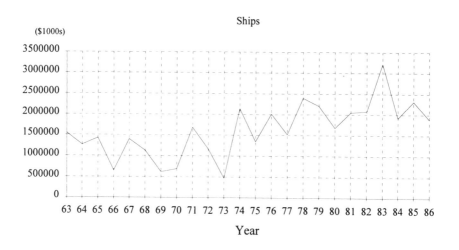

Ships

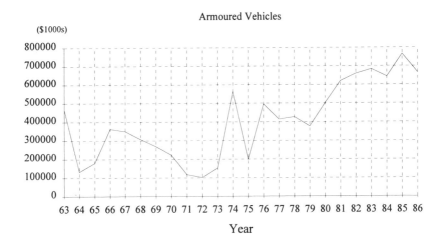

Armoured Vehicles

($1000s)

Year

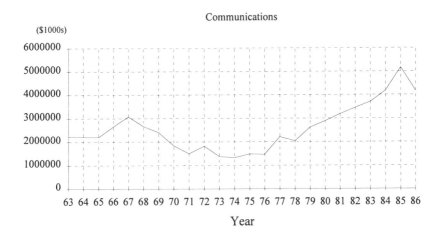

Communications

($1000s)

Year

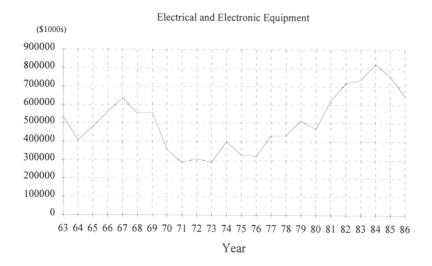

Electrical and Electronic Equipment

($1000s)

Year

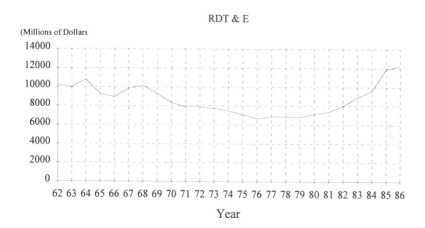

RDT & E

(Millions of Dollars

Year

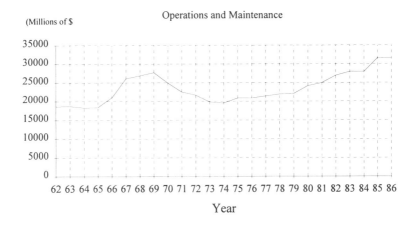

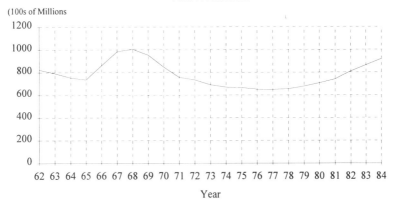

APPENDIX B

Affiliations of the Founding Board of Directors of the Committee on the Present Danger

Director Name	Organizational Ties
Theodore C. Achilles	Vice Chairman, Atlantic Council. Former Ambassador, Peru. Director, Eastman Kodak Co., International Management and Development Institute, NATO pact negotiator, Planning conference, CENTO, SEATO, and Columbo organizations. Co-editor, *Atlantic Community Journal* (63–75). Member of the Alibi, Yale, and Brook Clubs.
Richard V. Allen	President, Potomac International Company.
John M. Allison	Former Ambassador to Japan, Indonesia, and Czechoslovakia.
Eugenie Anderson	Former Ambassador to Denmark. Director, First National Bank of Minneapolis (71–75). Vice Chairman, Citizen's Committee for International Development. Co-Chairman, Minneapolis Commission for a Secure Middle East. Member, Democratic National Committee for Minnesota (48–9). Member

Director Name	Organizational Ties
	Democratic National Advisory Committee on Foreign Policy (57–71).
Eugene Bardach	Professor, University of California.
Frank R. Barnettb	President, National Strategy Information Center.
Joseph D. Baroody, Jr.	Public Affairs Consultant. Former Director of the American Enterprise Institute for Public Policy, Hoover Institute, and the Georgetown Center for Strategic and International Studies.
Jacob D. Beam	Former Ambassador to Poland, Czechoslovakia, and Soviet Union.
Saul Bellow	Author (Nobel Prize for Literature 1976).
Karl R. Bendetsen	Chairman of the Board of Directors, Panama Canal Company. Vice-President of Operations, Champion Paper. CEO, Chairman of the Board, President, Champion International. Director, Member of the Executive Committee, Westinghouse Electric, Governing Board, N.Y. Stock Exchange. Directed Evacuation of Japanese from the West Coast. Member of the Links, Metropolitan, Brook, Chicago, Washington Athletic, Bohemian, Pacific Union, Houston Country, Petroleum, Tejas, Bayou, Washington F Street,Georgetown, Everglades, and Bath and Tennis Clubs.
Joseph W. Bishop, Jr.	Professor, Yale University. Assistant to General Counsel, U.S. High Commission. Occupied Germany. Expert Counsel, SEC (1958). Member of the New Haven and Lawn Clubs.

Director Name	Organizational Ties
Adda B. Bozeman	Professor, Sarah Lawrence University. Post Graduate, Hoover Institute. Editorial Board, *Orbis, Asian Affairs.*
Donald G. Breenan	Director, National Security Studies, Hudson Institute.
Vincent J. Browne	Professor, Howard University.
W.Randolph Burgess	Former Under Secretary of Treasury and Ambassador to NATO.
John M. Cabot	Former Ambassador to Sudan, Colombia, Brazil, and Poland. Former Assistant Secretary of State for Inter-American Affairs
W. Glenn Campbell	Director, Hoover Institute. Advisory Board, Georgetown Center for Strategic and International Studies. Director, National Science Foundation. Regent, University of California. Member of the Bohemian Grove, Cosmos, and Commonwealth Clubs.
William J. Casey	Former Chair, SEC. Under Secretary of State. President of Export-Import Bank. Officer in the OSS. Founder, International Center for Economic Policy Studies.
Sol C. Chaikin	President of ILGWU. Member, Trilateral Commission.
Peter B. Clark	President of Evening News Association. Former Chairman, Federal Reserve Bank of Chicago. Member of Detroit Athletic, Detroit Country, and Economics Clubs.
Ray S. Cline	Director, Georgetown University Center for Strategic and International Studies. Officer in the OSS. Member of the Harvard Club of

Director Name	Organizational Ties
	N.Y.C. and the International Club in Washington D.C.
Edwin S. Cohen	Former Under Secretary of the Treasury. On "many advisory committees and boards." Consulting Lawyer to the IRS. Member of the Broad Street, Colonnade, Boars Head, and International Clubs.
William E. Colby	Former Director of the CIA. Former Attache to U.S. Embassy, Stockholm. Former Ambassador, Civil Ops and Rural Development, Saigon. Member of the Council on Foreign Relations. Member of the Cosmos, Princeton (NYC), Special Forces (London), and Linge Klubben (Oslo) Clubs.
John B. Connally	Former Secretary of the Treasury. Former Secretary of the Navy. Former Governor of Texas. Partner, Vinson and Elkins. Director, Justin Industries, Falconbridge Nickel Mines, Ltd., First City Bancorp of Texas, Inc., First City National Bank of Floresville, Continental Airlines, Inc, and Dr. Pepper Company. Trustee, Andrew W. Mellon Foundation. Member of the Houston Chamber of Commerce, and the Conference Board. Member and Director of the Houston Metropolitan Racquet Club.
William Connell	President, Concept Associates. Executive Assistant to Vice President Humphrey.
John T. Connor	President, Allied Chemical. Former Secretary of Commerce. Directors of J. Henry Schroeder Bank and Trust Co., G.M., ABC, Schroders Ltd, and Merck & Company. Member of the Business Council, and the

Director Name	Organizational Ties
	Council on Foreign Relations. Trustee, Syracuse University.
Colgate W. Darden, Jr.	Former President, University of Virginia.
Arthur H. Dean	Former-Chairman, U.S. Delegations on Nuclear Test Ban and Disarmament.
C. Douglas Dillon	Former Secretary of Treasury. Former Member of U.S. Stock Exchange. Former Director of U.S. and Foreign Securities Corporation. Director and Chair, Dillon, Reed, & Company. Former Chairman, Rockefellor Foundation. Former Trustee, Brookings Institute. President of Board of Overseers, Harvard University. Member of Society of Colonial Wars, New York. Member of Racquet and Tennis, Knickerbocker, Links, River, Century, Pilgrims, and Metropolitan Clubs.
S. Harrison Dogole	Chairman, Globe Security Systems.
Peter H. Dominick	Former U.S. Senator.
Walter Dowling	Former Ambassador, Germany.
Evelyn DuBrow	Legislative Director, ILGWU.
William DuChessi	Executive Vice President, Amalgamated Clothing and Textile Workers.
Valerie Earle	Professor, Georgetown University.
James T. Farrell	Author.
David Fellman	Professor, University of Wisconsin.
Henry H. Fowler	Partner, Goldman, Sachs & Company. Former Secretary of the Treasury. Vice Chairman, Atlantic Council. Member of the Conference Board. Member of the Recess

Director Name	Organizational Ties
	River (NYC), Links, and Metropolitan Clubs.
William H. Franklin	Former Chairman, Caterpillar Tractor Co.
Peter H. B. Frelinghuysen	Former Congressman, Investment Broker (NYC). Trustee, Howard Savings Bank.
Robert N. Ginsburgh	Major General, USAF (Ret.). Editor, *Strategic Review*. Former Research Fellow. Council on Foreign Relations, Neville Associates. Director, Drilling and Production Incorporated. Member of the Kenwood and International Clubs.
Nathan Glazer	Professor, Harvard University. Former Member and Staff, Communism in American Life Project, Fund for the Republic.
Andrew J. Goodpaster	General, U.S. Army (Ret.). Former NATO Commander. Former Chair, Atlantic Council of United States. Director, New York Life Insurance Company. Director, Bullock Funds. Trustee, George C. Marshall Foundation. Former Vice-President, International Institute for Strategic Studies. Member, Council on Foreign Relations. Member, University Club (NYC).
J. Peter Grace	President, W.R. Grace & Company. Director, Brascom Ltd, Ingorsoll-Rand Co., Stove and Webster, Inc., Omnicare, Roto Rooter Inc., Universal Furniture Ltd., and, Miliken & Company. Trustee, Atlantic Mutual Incorporated. Director, Boys Club of America. Chairman, Radio Free Europe. Trustee, Grace Institute. Member of Council on Foreign Relations. Member of Racquet and Tennis, Madison Square Garden, Links, India

Director Name	Organizational Ties
	House, Meadow Brook, Pacific Union, and Everglades Clubs.
Gordon Gray	Former President, University of North Carolina. Secretary of the Army.
Edmund A. Gullion	Dean, Fletcher School of Law and Diplomacy.
Barbara B. Gunderson	Former Civil Service Commissioner.
Oscar Handlin	Professor, Harvard University. Former Director, Center for the Study of Liberty in America. Member of the Colonial Society of Massachusetts.
John A. Hannah	Executive Director, United Nations World Food Council. Former Chairman, U.S. Commission on Civil Rights, and Administrator, AID.
David B. Harper	Gateway National Bank of St. Louis.
Huntington Harris	Trustee, The Brookings Institution.
Rita E. Hauser	Attorney, Stroock & Stroock & Lavan. Former Representative to the Human Rights Commission of the United States. Director, Wickes Companies Incorporated. Former Co-Chair, CREEP.
Donald C. Hellman	Professor, University of Washington.
Alfred C. Herrera	Research Associate, Johns Hopkins University, Washington Center of Foreign Policy Research.
Rachelle Horowitz	Director, Committee on Political Education, AFT.

Director Name	Organizational Ties
J.C. Hurewitz	Director, The Middle East Institute, Columbia University. Former researcher, Rand Corporation. Consultant to the Departments of State and Defense, Council on Foreign Relations, ABC News, Stanford Research Institute, and International Institute for Strategic Studies.
Belton K. Johnson	Chairman, Chaporrosa Agri-Services Incorporated. Former Manager, King Ranch, Texas. Director, Campbell Soup, ST&T, Tenneco, First City Bancorp of Texas. Former Director of Active Communication on Critical Choices for Americans. Former Co-Chair, Republican National Committee. Member of the Capital Hill, River, Racquet and Tennis, Clover Valley, Rod and Gun, Order of the Alamo, and Links Clubs.
Chalmers Johnson	Professor and Chairman, Department of Political Science, University of California.
Whittle Johnston	Professor, University of Virginia.
David C. Jordan	Professor and Chairman, Woodrow Wilson Department of Government, University of Virginia.
Max M. Kampelman	Attorney, Fried, Frank, Harris, Shriver & Kampelman. Chairman, Former Director, District of Columbia National Bank. Director, Georgetown University. Director, Atlantic Council. Member of the Cosmos, Federal City, and National Press Clubs.
Geoffrey Kemp	Professor, Fletcher School of Law and Diplomacy. Research Associate, Georgetown Center for Strategic and International Studies. Director, Council on Foreign Rela-

Director Name	Organizational Ties
	tions, International Institute for Strategic Studies. Member of the Oxford Union Society.
Leon H. Keyserling	President, Conference on Economic Progress. Chairman, Council of Economic Advisors under President Truman. Founder, Conference on Economic Progress. Director of "various companies". Member of the Cosmos, Harvard, and Columbia University (Washington, D.C.) Clubs.
Lane Kirkland	Secretary-Treasurer, AFL-CIO.
Jeane J. Kirkpatrick	Professor, Georgetown University. Former Director, Fund for the Republic. Resident Scholar, American Enterprise Institute for Public Policy. Member, Georgetown Center for Strategic and International Studies.
Foy K. Kohler	Professor, University of Miami. Former Ambassador to the Soviet Union. Former Director, Voice of America Broadcasts.
Peter Krogh	Dean, School of Foreign Service, Georgetown University.
Ernest W. Lefever	Professor, Georgetown University. Sr. Fellow, Foreign Policy Studies Brookings Institute. Editorial Board, *Policy Review.* Member of the International Institute for Strategic Studies. Council on Foreign Relations. Member, Cosmos and Yale Clubs.
Lyman L. Lemnitzer	General, U.S. Army (Ret.). Former Chairman, Joint Chiefs of Staffs, NATO Supreme Allied Commander, Europe.
Hobart Lewis	Chairman, Readers Digest.

Director Name	Organizational Ties
W.F. Libby	Former AEC Commissioner (Nobel Prize 1960 in Chemistry).
Sarason D. Liebler	President, Digital Recording Corporation.
James A. Linen IV	Director and former President of Time Incorporated. Executive Vice-President, *National Enquirer* (1976–7). Owner, Des Plaines Publishers. Vice-President, Media General Incorporated. CEO, Media General Broadcast Services Incorporated. Chairman of the Board, American Thai Corporation. Member, Economic, Racquet of Chicago, Round Hill, Country of Virginia, Commonwealth, Yale, Brook, and Farmington Country Clubs.
Seymour Martin Lipset	Professor, Stanford University. National Chairman, B'nai Brith Hillel Foundation. Member of the Cosmos Club.
Mary Pillsbury Lord	Former Representative to the Human Rights Commission of the United Nations.
Jay Lovestone	Consultant to AFL-CIO and ILGWU on International Affairs. Board of Directors, Atlantic Council, Council on Foreign Relations. Member, President's Labor advisory Council, and the National Planning Association.
Clare Boothe Luce	Author. Former Member of Congress. Ambassador to Italy. Member, Academy of Policy Science, American Institute for Foreign Trade. Director, American Security Council. Member, Hawaii's Foundation of American Freedom, U.S. Strategic Institute, and the Daughters of the American Revolution.

Director Name	Organizational Ties
John H. Lyons	President, Ironworkers International.
Donald S. MacNaughton	Chairman and CEO, The Prudential Insurance Company of America. CEO, Hospital Corp. of America. Chair, Executive Committee, Exxon Corporation. Director, Third National Corp., New York Stock Exchange. Trustee, Vanderbilt University. Member, Business Council. Member of the Eastward Ho, Sailfish Point, Links, and Belle Meade Clubs.
Leonard H. Marks	Former Director, United States Information Agency. Partner, Cohn and Marks. Chair of the Executive Committee, National Savings and Trust Company. Chair, International Conference on Communication Satellites. Member of the Cosmos, Metropolitan, Federal City, Broadcasters, and Alfalfa Clubs.
Charles Burton Marshall	Professor, Johns Hopkins University. Former Member, Policy Planning Staff, Department of State. Contributing Editor, National Review. Member, Council on Foreign Relations. Member of the Cosmos and Harvard Clubs.
William McChesney Martin, Jr.	Former Chairman, Federal Reserve Board. Member, New York Stock Exchange (31–38). Board of Directors, Import-Export Bank. Chair, Federal Reserve Board (51–70). Director, Freeport Minerals Co. and Scandinavian Securities Corporation. Member of the West Side Tennis, Yale, Metropolitan, Alibi, and Chevy Chase Clubs.

Director Name	Organizational Ties
Edward A. McCabe	Counsel to President Eisenhower. Director, First American Bank (Wash.), and USA Funds Incorporated. Chairman of the Board, Student Loan Marketing Association. Member of the Capital Hill, Metropolitan, Kenwood Golf and Country, and Burning Tree Clubs.
Samuel McCraken	Author.
George C. McGhee	Former Under Secretary of State for Public Affairs. Former Ambassador to Turkey. Owner, McGhee Production Co. (oil). Chairman of the Board, *Saturday Review*. Director, Mobil Corp., Procter & Gamble Co., American Security Bank, and Transworld Airlines. Member, Atlantic Council. Board of Directors, Vasser College, American University. Member of the Metropolitan, City Tavern, Brook, and Bohemenian Grove Clubs.
Robert E. McNair	Board of Directors, PBS. Member of the Masons, Shriners, and Lions Clubs.
John Miller	President, National Planning Association. Trustee, Member of the Advisory Conference on the Family.
George C. Mitchell	Executive Director, World Affairs Council of Pittsburgh.
Joshua M. Morse	Dean, College of Law, Florida State University.
Steven Muller	President, The Johns Hopkins University. Director, CSX Corp., Safeway Corp., Organization Counselors Inc., Millipore Corp. and Beneficial Corporation. Board of Editors,

Director Name	Organizational Ties
	Daedulus. Member of AAAS, Committee for Economic Development. Council on Foreign Relations, International Institute for Strategic Studies. Member of the Cosmos and Center Clubs.
Robert L. Mulliken	Professor, University of Chicago (Nobel Prize 1966 in Chemistry). Member of the NAS. Member, Cosmos Club.
Bess Myerson	Consumer Affairs Consultant, NYC. Former Commissioner of Consumer Affairs for NYC. Member of the Commission on Critical Choices.
Thomas S. Nichols	President, Nichols Company. Former Chairman, Executive Committee, Olin Corporation.
Paul H. Nitze	Chairman, Advisory Council, School of Advanced International Studies, John Hopkins University. Former Deputy Secretary of Defense. Partner, Dillon, Reed & Co. (1938–9).
William V. O'Brien	Chairman, Department of Government, Georgetown University.
George Olmsted	Chairman and CEO, International Bank, Washington, D.C. Chairman, First Insurance and Finance Co., United Security Insurance Company. Director, Northeastern Insurance Co., Hawkeye Insurance Co., United Security Insurance Co., International General Industries Inc., General Service Life Co., and Bankers Security Life Company. Founder, United Federal Savings and Loan Association. Chairman, I.B. Credit

Director Name	Organizational Ties
	Corporation, Avis Industrial Corp, Woodman Co., and Kliklok Corp. NYC. Member of the Shriners, Metropolitan, Army-Navy and Washington Golf and Country Clubs.
David Packard	Chairman of the Board, Hewlett-Packard Company. Former Deputy Secretary of Defense. Director, Gentech, Boeing Co., Member, Trilateral Commission, Atlantic Council, American Enterprise Institute for Public Policy. Board of Overseers, Hoover Institute, Business Roundtable. Trustee, Herbert Hoover Foundation, Stanford University. Member of the Bohemian Grove, Commonwealth, Pacific Union, Worldtrade, Links, Alfalfa, Capital Hill, and California Clubs.
James L. Payne	Professor, Texas A&M University.
Robert L. Pfaltzgraff, Jr.	Professor, Fletcher School of Law and Diplomacy. President, U.S. Strategic Institute (77–79). Member of the Council on Foreign Relations and International Institute for Strategic Studies. Member of the America Club (London).
Midge Decter Podhoretz	Author and Editor. Managing Editor, *Commentary*. Editor, Hudson Institute. Executive Director, Committee for a Freeworld. Board of Directors, Heritage Foundation. Advisory Board, Radio Broadcasting to Cuba. Member of the Council on Foreign Relations.
Norman Podhoretz	Editor, *Commentary*. Member of the Council on Foreign Relations and the Committee for the Free World.

Director Name	Organizational Ties
Uri Ra'anan	Professor and Chairman of the International Security Studies Program, Fletcher School of Law and Diplomacy.
Estelle R. Ramey	Professor, Georgetown School of Medicine.
Paul Ramsey	Professor, Princeton University.
Matthew B. Ridgeway	General, U.S. Army (Ret.). Former Chief of Staff, U.S. Army.
John P. Roche	Professor, Fletcher School of Law and Diplomacy. Special Consultant to President Johnson. National Chairman, Americans for Democratic Action. Executive Committee, Civil Liberties Union of Massachusetts. Member, National Council on Humanities. Trustee, Woodrow Wilson Center for Scholars, Smithsonian Institution. Member of the Hudson Institute, Council on Foreign Relations. Member of the Cosmos, and St. Batolph Clubs.
H. Chapman Rose	Former Under Secretary of the Treasury. Board of Directors, Atlantic Council. Trustee Emeritus, Princeton University, Brookings Institute. Member of the Union, Tavern, Kirkland Country, Princeton, Metropolitan, Burning Tree and Chevy Chase Clubs.
Peter R. Rosenblatt	Associate, Stroock & Stroock & Lavan. Chairman, Executive Committee, Coalition for a Democratic Majority.
Eugene V. Rostow	Professor of Law, Yale Law School. Former Under Secretary of State for Political Affairs. President, Atlantic Treaty Association. Advisor Dept. of State 1942–1944. Member of

Director Name	Organizational Ties
	the Elizabethan (Yale), Lawn (NYC), Century, Association, and Cosmos Clubs.
James H. Rowe, Jr.	Administrative Assistant to President Roosevelt.
Dean Rusk	Professor, School of Law, The University of Georgia. Former Under Secretary of State for Administration. Former President of the Rockefeller Foundation.
Bayard Rustin	President, A Phillip Randolph Institute. Organizer, March on Washington for Jobs and Freedom. Chairman, Social Democrats, USA. Board of Directors, NAACP Legal Defense Fund. Member, Black Americans to Support Israel Committee, Coalition for a Democratic Majority. Board of Directors, Freedom House.
Charles E. Saltzman	Partner, Goldman, Sachs & Company. Former Under Secretary of State for Administration. Partner, Henry Sears and Co. (49–56). Member, English Speaking Union of the U.S. (pres. 61–66). Member of the University, Union, Downtown Association, Century Association, and Pilgrim Clubs.
Richard Mellon Scaife	Publisher, *Tribune-Review*. Director, Sarah Scaife Foundation.
Richard Schifter	Attorney, Fried, Frank, Harris, Shriver & Kampelman. Member, Montgomery County Democratic Central Committee. Chairman, Maryland Governor's commission on Funding Education of the Handicapped.
Paul Seabury	Professor, University of California.

Director Name	Organizational Ties
Albert Shanker	President, American Federation of Teachers. Board of Directors, A. Phillip Randolph Institute. Member, NYC Council for Economic Education, Committee for a Free World, and the Trilateral Commission.
Milan B. Skacel	President, Chamber of Commerce of Latin America in the U.S.A.
Fred Smith	Chairman, Board of Trustees, National Planning Association. Former Assistant to the Secretary of the Treasury.
Lloyd H. Smith	President, Paraffin Oil Corporation. Vice President, Argus Research Corporation. Executive Director, City National Bank Houston. Director, National Review, Curtiss-Wright Corp., Info Storage Systems, Falcon Seaboard Incorporated. Trustee, Pine Mountain College. Member of the Bayou, Ramada, Tejas, Everglades, Racquet and Tennis, Brook, River, National Golf, Links, Southampton, and Meadow Clubs.
Kenneth Spang	International Business Adviser, Citibank.
Ralph I. Straus	Director, Atlantic Council of the U.S.
Harold W. Sweatt	Former Chairman of the Board, Honeywell, Inc.
George K. Tanham	Vice-President and Trustee, The Rand Corporation. Associate Director, AID, Saigon. Director, Crane & Rusack Co. Incorporated. Member, Council on Foreign Relations, International Institute for Strategic Studies. Member of the Cosmos, Union, Andirondack League, and Middlebury Tennis Association Clubs.

Director Name	Organizational Ties
Gobart Taylor, Jr.	Former Director, Export-Import Bank.
Maxwell D. Taylor	General U.S. Army (Ret.). Former Chairman, Joint Chiefs of Staff and Chief of Staff, U.S. Army.
Edward Teller	Professor Emeritus, University of California. Sr. Researcher, Hoover Institution. Board of Directors, Association to Unite the Democracies. Sponsor, Atlantic Union, Atlantic Council, University Centers for Rational Alternatives, Member, Committee to Unite America, Inc.
Arthur Temple	Chairman of the Board, President and C.E.O., Temple-Eastex Inc.
J.C. Turner	General President, International Union of Operating Engineers. Vice-President, Member of the Executive Council, AFL-CIO, 1975–85. Vice Chair, District of Columbia Democratic Central Committee. Member of the D.C. City Council. Trustee, National Urban League. Vice-President, Board of Governors. Chair, Executive Committee, United Way. President, American for Energy Independence. Member, National Planning Association. Member of the National Democratic, National Press, and Touchdown Clubs.
Charles Tyroler, II	President, Quadri-Science Incorporated. Former Director of Manpower Supply, Dept. of Defense.
William R. Van Cleave	Professor, University of Southern California. Fellow, Center for the Study of the American Experience. Chairman, Strategic Alternatives Team. Member, Advisory

Director Name	Organizational Ties
	Council on National Security to the Republican National Committee. Research Council, Foreign Policy Research Institute. Sr. Fellow, Hoover Institute. Board of Editors, *Orbis, International Security Review,* and *Global Affairs.* Member of the International Institute for Strategic Studies.
Charles E. Walker	Charles E. Walker Associates, Incorporated. Former Deputy Secretary of the Treasury. Vice President, Republic National Bank, Dallas. Executive Vice President, Bankers Association, NYC. Director, Enron Corp., Potomac Electric Power Co., Tracor Inc., and USF & G Corporation. Chairman, American Council for Capital Formation. Co-Chairman, Bretton Woods Committee. Member, Council on Foreign Relations. Member of the Union League, Burning Tree, and Congressional Clubs.
Marin J. Ward	President, Plumbers' and Pipe Fitters' International Union.
Robert E. Ward	Director, Center for Research on International Studies, Stanford University. Member, National Council, National Endowment for the Humanities. Chairman, SSRC (69–71).
Paul S. Weaver	President, Lake Erie College.
Richard J. Whalen	Author and Journalist. Associate Editor, *Fortune Magazine.* Sr. Edit. (62–66). Editorial Writer, *Wall Street Journal.* Writer in Residence, Georgetown Center for Strategic Studies (later the Center for Strategic and

Director Name	Organizational Ties
	International Studies). Member of the Council on Foreign Relations and the Cosmos Club.
Eugene P. Wigner	Theoretical Physicist, Princeton University,(Nobel Prize 1963 in Physics). Member, General Advisory Commission to the Atomic Energy Commission.
Francis O. Wilcox	Director General, Atlantic Council of the United States. Former Assistant, Secretary of State. Chief of Staff, Senate Foreign Relations Committee.
Bertram D. Wolfe	Professor Emeritus, University of California. Senior Research Fellow, Hoover Institution, Stanford University.
Elmo R. Zumwalt	Admiral, U.S.N. (Ret.). Former Chief of Naval Operations. Public Governor, American Stock Exchange. Chairman, Phelps-Stokes Fund. Director, Esmark Inc., Transway International, RMI Inc., American Building, Maintenance Industries, Navistar International Corp., Gifford-Hill & Co., and Unicomp America. CEO, President, American Medical Buildings Incorporated. President, Admiral Zumwalt and Associates.

[a]Adapted from Shoup (1980) and Sanders (1983), Affiliations from *(Who's Who in America) (1982, 1988)
[b]"Individuals with direct affiliations with New Right foundations and thinktanks described by Himmelstein (1990) and Allen (1989, 1987) are underlined.

NOTES

1. Research on the U.S. Military

1. In 1982 the United States had a minimum of 7,236 strategic nuclear warheads and the Soviet Union a maximum of 9,745 strategic nuclear warheads available. Just before the collapse of the Soviet Union the estimated number of Soviet warheads had increased 28 percent to 11,159, the U.S. arsenal had increased 35 percent to 9,745 (International Institute for Strategic Studies 1992:219–220).

2. A more recent revised version of this document softens much of the call for the United States to be the only superpower. It is explicit, however, in emphasizing that we must ". . . preclude any hostile power from dominating a region critical to our interests." (April 16, 1992 draft of *Defense Planning Guidance for the 1994–1999 fiscal years*)

3. It is important to note that when expenditures from trust funds such as social security are included as part of welfare expenditures, the federal government committed more of the GNP to welfare and social insurance than to national security beginning in 1972. Also note that most government compiled aggregate data on expenditures began to include some trust fund expenditures in 1968 and all Social Security and other off-budget expenditures by the mid-1970s.

4. Most of the case studies of weapons rely explicitly or implicitly on organizational politics paradigms to guide their research.

5. Note that I do not mean to slight the excellent scholarship contained in most of these works. Rather, I want to indicate the differences in style and emphasis between this body of literature and some of the other literatures relating to the military.

6. A search of NOTIS library listings turns up eleven books published between 1970 and 1975 using some form of military-industrial complex perspective. For 1976 to 1990 there are only four books listed. The *Social Sciences and Humanities Index* indicates that the peak years of listings under the military-industrial complex subject heading were 1971 to 1976 with eighteen articles listed and 1987 to 1992 with fifteen listed.

7. Many aspects of elite theory are very much rooted in the work of Max Weber, but few elite theory scholars trumpet these roots.

8. For the years 1963 through 1972 the government document containing these series, *Prime Military Contract Awards by Service Category and Federal Supply Classification,* is apparently only available on microfiche from this service. For 1973 through 1976 the document is available only in printed form, and for 1977 to the present the document is available in both printed form and on microfiche from Congressional Information Service.

9. For the late 1970s to date the data source I use here, *Prime Military Contract Awards by Service Category and Federal Supply Classification,* provides very fine subclassifications for procurement expenditures. For example, the volume containing data for 1984–1987 breaks the category for weapons into fifteen subcategories including guns, through 30 millimeters, guns, over 30 millimeters up to 75 millimeters, chemical weapons and equipment, degaussing and mine sweeping equipment and miscellaneous weapons. Overall, in this volume there are over three hundred subclassifications, some listing as little as $25,000 in expenditures for one year.

10. Other categories include such things as fuels and lubricants, aircraft components, and weapons components.

11. I did not use fuels and lubricants because these expenditures are extremely dependent on the price of oil. Thus, any statistical relationships that I might find would be extremely difficult to interpret.

12. U.S. and South Vietnamese forces used huge quantities of defoliants during the war to reduce cover available to North Vietnamese, Viet Cong, Viet Minh, and allied forces; to construct landing areas; and to destroy food crops in North Vietnam. All totaled, operations RANCH HAND and FARMGATE, along with several smaller defoliation operations, covered 5,229,484 acres with 2,4,5 T (Agent Orange, so named because of the color markings on the containers) and the less widely used Agent Blue (Lewy 1978: 258–260).

13. I use this term to refer to fully state-centered models as well as models positing some significant constraints on the autonomy of the state. These models include the overlapping theories relating to electoral politics, budgetary politics, and bureaucratic politics as well as the state-centered approach posited by Skocpol and her students.

2. Defense Contractor Politics and Profit

1. There is quality research in this area; there is just not that much material that uses similar methods and that is similarly systematic.

2. However, for many contemporary defense firms the U.S. government is but one of several markets for their products, albeit by far the largest. In the middle 1970s almost 40 percent of arms sales of U.S. firms were to other nations. By the middle 1980s the proportion had fallen to less than 20 percent. There is now a buyers market for weapons (Gansler 1989). Also note that a very large percentage of U.S. firms' overseas sales are organized, promoted, and initiated by the Pentagon or the Department of State. This is especially true of large weapons sales such as AWACS, F-16s, and armored vehicles. Thus, even when the ultimate consumer of weapons is not the United States, it plays central roles in the arms transactions.

3. The formal title of the Finletter Commission was the Air Policy Board. Thomas Finletter was the chair of the commission. Several scholars conclude that this com-

mission, consisting mostly of corporate liberals, was very influential both because of the commission's publications and because of the political action of its individual members (Domhoff 1970; Pursell 1972; Yergin 1978).

4. Obvious and significant design defects in the C-5A's wings made it necessary for the C-5B modification. According to Robert Ormsby, president of Lockheed Georgia, "Without the wing modification contract Lockheed's growth curve for the early 1980s would have been 'flat'" (Stubbing and Mendel 1986).

5. Chrysler, the maker of armored vehicles and some electronics, made the M-1 tank until it sold the subsidiary making armored vehicles to General Dynamics in the mid-1980s.

6. Since defense contracting requires a firm to bear heavy bureaucratic, political and sometimes economic burdens, the state must make special efforts not only to ensure that defense contractors will not defect to non-defense markets, but also to ensure that when significant expansion in the demand for war materials is underway, new firms can be recruited into the fold of defense suppliers.

7. Usually Congress cuts the funding for this project to between $3 and $5.5 billion. Despite Clinton's avowed desire to cut the budget of the military, his 1993 budget contained over $2 billion for this program.

8. Initially the Minuteman I, the first U.S. solid-fueled ICBM, was slated to be a mobile missile. The missile was to be moved around in climate-controlled railroad cars on the existing railway system. Problems of warhead accuracy and security proved terminal for this proposal (interview with Isaac C. Boies, engineer on Minuteman project from 1965 to 1982).

9. See Mayhew's (1974) discussion of the "casework" members of Congress do for constituents. The role of the "Keating Five" is an excellent example of the nature of "casework" done for corporate constituents.

3. Elite Social Movement Organizing and Defense Policy

1. Other studies examining the influence of social movements on public policy and on major social institutions include Gamson (1975), Tarrow (1983), Holland and Hoover (1985).

2. In 1950 the first Committee on the Present Danger was founded. This committee was very similar to the CPD I describe here.

3. For example, John Cabot's brother, Thomas D. Cabot, was on the board of directors of United Fruit Company while John was Secretary of State for Inter-American Affairs (March 1953 to March 1954). Coincidentally, this was also the period when the United States intervened in Guatemala against the Arbenz regime. Apparently John Cabot was remarkably hostile toward the Arbenz regime after they had nationalized United Fruit's holding in Guatemala. For more on this see Cole Blasier, *The Hovering Giant: U.S. Responses to Revolutionary Change in Latin America* (Pittsburgh: University of Pittsburgh Press, 1976), 160–164.

4. During this time Norman and Midge Decter Podhoretz, influential CPD directors, edited *Commentary* (*Who's Who in America* 1983). *Commentary* became the intellectual forum for containment militarism, much as *Foreign Policy* did for trilateralism during the 1960s (Sanders 1983).

5. Primarily these numbers are used to calculate single-shot kill probability and other relevant estimates of a nuclear arsenal's capability. The equation for kill probability is:

$$P_{kill} = 1 - e^{-R2/S2}$$

where R = 2.9 (warhead yield/silo hardness)$^{1/3}$ and S = (.85*CEP). CEP is a measure of warhead accuracy in miles, yield is in megatons, silo hardness in pounds per square inch dynamic blast overpressure. See Tsipsis (1983) and Craig and Jungerman (1986) for more details. P_{kill} is especially sensitive to missile accuracy and less sensitive to warhead yield and silo hardness.

6. Using special ties to the media to further the political interests of upper-class organizations is not new. During the New Deal the corporate liberals used the media extensively to pressure President Roosevelt and other top decisionmakers (Domhoff 1991:10–11).

7. C. W. Mills would certainly not have been the least bit surprised that an organization such as this one would form. To him the CPD would be unique not because it consisted mainly of members of the power elite, but because it was primarily an impermanent social movement organization rather than an institutionalized policy discussion organization like the Council on Foreign Relations.

8. Tyroler's (1984) edited volume of CPD major publications ". . . contains all of the publications of the Committee on the Present Danger from its inception on 11 November 1976 to this writing" [October 1984, xiii]. There are two publications from 1976, two from 1977, three from 1978, six from 1979, two from 1980, two from 1982, and two from 1984 listed in the table of contents. These publications do not exhaust the list of books, articles, and reports authored by members and directors of the CPD, but they do contain most of the core ideology and policy recommendations of the committee.

9. John Prados (1986) indicates that Ronald Reagan's administration covertly and overtly supported many right-wing movements around the world. The Department of State has estimated that during the early 1980s as many as 100,000 people were killed and over 250,000 made into refugees as a result of just one covertly supported war in Mozambique.

10. The amount of time passing before the effects of CPD activity appear in increased expenditures will vary both between weapons categories and even within weapons categories because each hardware category has different lag times from the decision to purchase and the actual disbursement of money to contractors. Extensive analysis indicates that CPD activity lagged two years provides the best performing ordinary least squares estimates for all expenditure models with the sole exception of guided missiles. This model did best with CPD activity lagged three years.

4. Theories of the State and the Military

1. In general, while most budgetary theorists are very explicit about budget-cutting or -spending, "moods" or "trends" being central to understanding policy-making processes, there is little attempt to explicitly and precisely define this concept.

These "moods" appear to be a residual category for political changes that are not directly linked to international competitions and are not explained by the budgetary politics model.

2. Skocpol's most recent book, *Protecting Soldiers and Mothers* (1992, Harvard University Press) evolves her state-centered theory into a more clearly traditional pluralist argument (see Domhoff's 1993 review, "The Death of State Autonomy Theory: A Review of Skocpol's *Protecting Soldier and Mothers*").

3. While this is central to the state-centered scholars' work on New Deal policy, it has yet to be applied to the military.

4. Albeit the planning comes solely in the form of paying defense contractors in the aircraft and a few other sectors to develop what national security planners felt was good for national security. In a few cases, once World War II was over, the government would make direct capital investments to build plants and facilities when defense contractors were unable or unwilling to do so. The Department of Defense then gave these facilities to the contractors, often for one dollar.

5. This is not inconsistent with the preponderance of research examining the effect the defense expenditures of the Soviet Union on the U.S. military budget decisions. The most recent research concludes that there is little evidence indicating that U.S. military expenditures are in any way dependent on those of the former Soviet Union (Nincic 1982; Nincic and Cusock 1979; Griffin, Devine, Wallace 1982a; Davis and Powell 1987).

6. Paul Baran and Paul Sweezy (1966) initially articulated this model and Larry Griffin and his colleagues (Griffin, Devine, and Wallace 1982a; 1982b) applied it to defense spending particularly well.

7. This is especially true for the monopoly capital theorists. James O'Connor (1973) also emphasizes military expenditures and military Keynesianism as important features of the U.S. central state.

8. For example, the 1976 book value of U.S. direct foreign investment abroad was $137 billion, up from $75 billion in 1970, $31 billion in 1960, and only $11.6 billion in 1950 (Economic Report of the President, 1978). Note, however, that these figures are not adjusted for inflation and thus overstate the increases in direct investment abroad. Direct investment abroad by U.S. firms was $232 billion by 1985. (*The World Almanac and Book of Facts: 1987*. NY: Random House Inc.) Foreign investment by U.S. manufacturing firms was 31 percent of their domestic investment in 1974, compared to only 21 percent at the end of the 1960s. (Andrew J. Biemiller, before the Senate Subcommittee on Multinational Corporations of the Senate Committee on Foreign Relations on the Impact of Multinational Corporations on the U.S. Economy, December 10, 1975)

9. Indeed, much of the state-centered literature on the New Deal strongly emphasizes the importance of having a Democratically controlled Congress to the formation of many New Deal policies (for example, see Skocpol and Amenta 1985; Skocpol and Finegold 1990; Orloff and Skocpol 1984)

10. It is important to remember, however, that there have been some important fluctuations in expenditures for most categories of expenditures.

11. For the years 1985 and 1986 I estimated the rate of profit based on data contained in one of Dumenil, Glick, and Rangel's original sources, *Survey of Current Business.*

5. The Results

1. In recent years there are well over three hundred sub-categories of procurement expenditures and more than a hundred major categories. In the nine major categories I use here, there are usually twenty to thirty-five sub-categories of expenditures. For example, for the fiscal years 1984 through 1987 the document breaks expenditures on aircraft into expenditures on fixed-wing, rotary-wing, gliders, drones, and airframe structural components.

2. McCleary and Hays (1980:99) describe this statistic.

3. One possible cause of these problems could be model misspecification. There may exist a nonlinear relationship between some of these variables and some of the dependent variables. I tested some models with nonlinear specifications, but did not find any positive change in the results. I did not, however, test all variables in all possible ways. That project remains on the list of additional analyses for these data. I must add here that because one of the major effects of autocorrelation is to inflate the t-ratios used to test the significance of the regression coefficients, it is very likely that if these problem variables had any significant influence on the dependent variables the t-tests would have been statistically significant.

4. Normally lagging one of the variables two years rather than one year will reduce the sample size by one additional case. For this analysis that would mean only twenty-three valid cases for analysis. However, during the first thirteen years of this time series, the value for CPD activity was zero. Thus, I could just add as many zeros as necessary to the beginning of the data file.

5. Much of the increasing capabilities showing up in modern weapons systems, especially ships, aircraft, and missiles, stem from increasingly expensive and sophisticated electronics (Friedman et al. 1985; Bonds 1983; Hudson and Kruzel 1985). The flight performance of modern aircraft, for example the F-15, is only somewhat better than previous generation aircraft such as the F-4 Phantom, but the ability of the F-15 to find and destroy targets as well as evade detection and destruction is vastly superior to the F-4. This increased capability is largely the result of the F-15's very sophisticated electronics (Gansler 1989; Gervasi 1981; Kaldor 1981).

6. Assessing the Results

1. In analyses that I do not report here defense profitability is positively related to the size of the military procurement expenditures.

2. People from these two companies have been very active in politics since the New Deal era. Officials of these firms have been on the Business Advisory Council, War Projects Board, National Recovery Act's Industrial Advisory Board, as well as holding positions in government such as ambassador to France (1953–1957), Secretary of the Navy (1947–1949), and Undersecretary of the Navy (1940–1944) (Burch 1980).

3. Ideally, to properly examine the relative viability of the proposed hypotheses I should examine them using two-staged least squares or better yet a causal model analysis program such as Lisrel or EQS. Unfortunately, the complexities of the relationships this book examines require a very complex causal model. Even if I had data for every year since World War II, I would not have enough cases to properly estimate the required models.

4. *Business Week* analysts concluded in the mid-1980s "No industry has caused more banks to fall from grace in 1980s than oil." Quoted in Mikdashi 1986.

5. For many U.S. defense firms the second or third largest market for their weapons is the Middle East. The world arms trade generated an average of about $20.5 billion per year (1985 dollars) in gross income for U.S. firms for 1981–1985, about 19 percent of that coming from the Middle East, the largest single market for U.S. arms (ACDA 1988; Bajusz and Louscher 1988).

6. In addition to using Limdep, I also tested the models appearing in this document, with Shazam (White et al. 1988). The Durbin's h statistic calculated by Shazam for models with lagged dependent variables indicated little problem with autocorrelation. This statistic, which Limdep does not compute, is one of several appropriate methods to test for autocorrelation in OLS models with lagged dependent variables (Judge et al. 1980; White et al. 1988)

7. Kessler and Greenberg (1981) suggest that including a lagged dependent variable in a regression analysis can be interpreted as making the model into an analysis of change scores rather than of static scores, a third approach to the meaning of lagged dependent variables.

8. Diego Garcia is now an important military base complete with major naval facilities, large stores of prepositioned war material, an air base capable of handling B-52s and smaller aircraft, plus it is a base for high speed roll-on–roll-off transport ships.

9. This criticism is focused primarily on research surrounding New Deal policy, but it is readily leveled at other policy issues as well. Indeed, Hooks (1990) seems to be making this a central point in his argument about state-building after World War II.

10. State-centric theorists apply this label to almost all models giving dominance over the state in the formation of social policy to corporations, members of the upper class, or business leaders. The work of G. William Domhoff (1970, 1983, 1987, 1990) Gabriel Kolko (1963), and Michael Useem (1983) are often included in this category of theory and research. Jill Quadagno (1984) has also significantly advanced to this perspective (1984). Other researchers following this line of theory include Jenkins and Brents (1989) and Akard (1992).

REFERENCES CITED

Adams, Gordon. 1981. *The Iron Triangle*. New York: The Council on Economic Priorities.

Adams, Walter. 1968. "The Military-Industrial Complex and the New Industrial State." *American Economic Review* 58(May).

Aldridge, Robert. C. 1983. *First Strike! The Pentagon's Strategy for Nuclear War*. Boston: South End Press.

Akard, Pat. 1992. "Corporate Mobilization and Political Power: The Transformation of U.S. Economic Policy in the 1970s." *American Sociological Review* 57:597–615.

Aldridge, Robert C. 1978. *The Counterforce Syndrome*. Washington, D.C.: The Institute for Policy Studies.

Alford, Robert R. 1975. "Paradigms of Relations Between State and Society." In L. N. Lindberg, R. R. Alford, C. Crouch, and C. Offe (eds.), *Stress and Contradiction in Modern Capitalism*. Lexington, Mass.: Lexington Books.

Allen, Michael Patrick. 1992. "Elite Social Movement Organizations and the State: The Rise of the Conservative Policy-Planning Network." In Gwen Moore and J. Allen Whitt (eds.), *The Political Consequences of Social Networks*, Vol. 4 of Research in Politics and Society. Greenwich, Conn.: JAI Press (87–110).

Allen, Michael Patrick. 1987. *The Founding Fortunes: A New Anatomy of the Super-Rich Families in America*. New York: Truman Tally Books.

Annual Report of the President. 1981. *Federal Advisory Committees*. Washington, D.C.: Government Printing Office.

Armacost, M. H. 1969. *The Politics of Weapons Innovation: The Thor-Jupiter Controversy*. New York: Columbia University Press.

Art, R. J. 1974a. "The Military-Industrial Complex: Arms Control in Institutional Perspective." *Public Policy* 22:423–459.

Art, R. J. 1974b. "Why We Overspend and Under Accomplish: Weapons Procurement and the Military-Industrial Complex," in S. Rosen (ed.), *Testing Theories of the Military-Industrial Complex*. Lexington, Mass.: D. C. Heath and Co.

Ashford, Kathryn L. 1986. "The Role of Corporations in the 1980 U.S. Congressional Elections." *Sociological Inquiry* 56 (Fall):409–431.

Axelrod, Daniel, Justin Schwartz, and John Boies. 1986. *Weapons in Space: Peace on Earth?*. Ann Arbor: Michigan Alliance for Disarmament.

Bajusz, William D., and David J. Louscher. 1988. *Arms Sales and The U.S. Economy*. Boulder, Colo.: Westview Press.

Ball, N. and M. Leitenberg. 1983. *The Structure of the Defense Industry, An International Survey*. London: Croom Helm.

Ball, D. 1980. *Politics and Force Levels: The Strategic Missile Program of the Kennedy Administration*. Berkeley: University of California Press.

Baran, P., and P. Sweezy. 1966. *Monopoly Capital*. New York: Monthly Review Press.

Barnet, Richard J. 1971. *Roots of War*. New York: Atheneum.

Barnet, Richard J., and Ronald E. Muller. 1974. *Global Reach: The Power of the Multinational Corporation*. New York: Simon and Schuster.

Beach, C. and J. Mackinnon. 1978. "A Maximum Likelihood Procedure for Regression with Autocorrelated Errors." *Econometrica* 46:51–58.

Beard, E. 1976. *Developing the ICBM, A Study in Bureaucratic Politics*. New York: Columbia University Press.

Betts, R. K., ed. 1981. *Cruise Missile, Technology, Strategy, and Politics*. Washington, D.C.: Brookings Institute.

Blair, John M. 1976. *The Control of Oil*. New York: Random House, Vintage Books.

Block, Fred 1977a. "Beyond Corporate Liberalism." *Social Problems* 24:352–361.

Block, Fred. 1977b. The Ruling Class Does Not Rule: Notes on the Marxist Theory of the State." *Socialist Revolution* 33:6–28.

Block, Fred. 1987. *Revising State Theory: Essays in Politics and Postindustrialism*. Philadelphia: Temple University Press.

Bobrow, D. B., ed. 1969. *Weapons Systems Decisions: Political and Psychological Perspectives on Continental Defense*. New York: Praeger.

Boies, John L. 1989. "Money, Business, and the State: Material Interests, Fortune 500 Corporations, and the Size of Political Action Committees." *American Sociological Review* 54:821–833.

Bonds, R. 1983. *The United States War Machine: An Encyclopedia of American Military Equipment and Strategy*. New York: Crown.

Brennan, Donald G. 1975. *Arms Treaties with Moscow: Unequal Terms Unevenly Applied*. Washington, D.C.: National Strategic Information Center.

Bright, Charles. 1978. *The Jet Makers: The Aerospace Industry from 1945 to 1972*. Lawrence: The Regents Press of Kansas.

Burch, Philip H., Jr. 1980. *Elites in History: The New Deal to the Carter Administration*. New York: Holmes & Meier Publishers.

Burris, Val. 1992. "Elite Policy-Planning Networks in the United States." *Research in Politics and Society* 4:111–134.

Burt, R. 1974/5. *Defence Budgeting: The British and American Cases*. Adelphi Paper #112, Wtr.

Cannizzo, C. 1980. *The Gun Merchants*. New York: Pergamon Press.

Chappell, Henry. 1981. "Campaign Contribution and Voting on the Cargo Preference Bill: A Comparison of Simultaneous Models." *Public Choice* 36:301–312.

Chatterjee, P. 1974. "Equilibrium Theory of Arms Races: Some Extensions." *Journal of Peace Research* 11(3):203–211.

Chester, E. 1978. "Military Spending and Capitalist Stability." *Cambridge Journal of Economics*. 2(September):293–298.

Christian Science Monitor. 1979. "Anti-Salt Lobbyists Outspend Pros 15 to 1." March 23, 1979, 1.

Clawson, Dan, Alan Neustadtl, and James Bearden. 1986. "The Logic of Business Unity: Corporate Contributions to the 1980 Congressional Elections." *American Sociological Review* 51(December):797–811.

Clayton, J. L. 1976. "Fiscal Limits of the Warfare-Welfare State: Defense and Welfare Spending in the United States since 1900." *Political Quarterly* 29:364–383.

Cliff, Norman. 1987. *Analyzing Multivariate Data.* New York: Harcourt Brace Jovanovich.

Cline, William R. 1983. *International Debt and the Stability of the World Economy.* Washington D.C.: Institute for International Economics.

Cobb, Stephen. 1976. "Defense Spending and Defense Voting in the House." *American Journal of Sociology* 82(July):163–183.

Cobb, Stephen. 1973. "The United States Senate and the Impact of Defense Spending Concentrations" in S. Rosen (ed.), *Testing Theories of the Military Industrial Complex.* Lexington, Mass. D. C. Heath and Co.

Cobb, Stephen. 1968. *The TFX Decision: MacNamara and the Military.* Boston: Little Brown.

Collins, John M. 1978. *American and Soviet Military Trends Since the Cuban Missile Crisis.* Washington, D.C.: The Center for Strategic and International Studies, Georgetown University.

Collins, John M. 1982. *U.S. Defense Planning: A Critique.* Boulder, Colo.: Westview Press.

Committee on the Present Danger. 1985. *Can America Catch Up? The United States-Soviet Military Balance.* Washington, D.C.: Committee on the Present Danger.

Committee on the Present Danger. 1981. *The Fifth Year . . . and the New Administration.* Washington, D.C.: Committee on the Present Danger.

Common Cause. 1989. *Common Cause.* (March):23–27.

Coolidge, Cathleen and Gordon Tullock. 1980. "Firm Size and Political Power" in John Siegfried (ed.), *The Economics of Firm Size, Market Structure, and Social Responsibility.* Washington, D.C.: Government Printing Office, 43–71.

Cooling, Benjamin F. 1979. *Gray Steel and Blue Water Navy: The Formative Years of America's Military-Industrial Complex.* Hamden, Conn.: Archon Books.

Coulam, R. F. 1977. *Illusions of Choice: the F111 and the Problems of Weapons Acquistion Reform.* Princeton: Princeton University Press.

Craig, Paul P. and John A. Jungerman. 1986. *Nuclear Arms Race: Technology and Society.* New York: McGraw-Hill.

Crecine, J. P. 1979. *Defense Budgeting: Organizational Adaptation to External Constraints.* Santa Monica: The Rand Corporation.

Cuff, R. D. 1978. "An Organizational Perspective on the Military-Industrial Complex." *Business History Review* 52(2):250–261.

Cushman, John H., Jr. 1988. *The New York Times.* May 13, 1988.

Dahl, R. 1961. *Who Governs? Democracy and Power in an American City.* New Haven, Conn.: Yale University Press.

Davis, Gerald F., and Walter W. Powell. 1987. "Organizations and the Arms Race: Accounting for Escalation," unpublished.

Degolyer and MacNaughton. 1989. *Twentieth-Century Petroleum Statistics: 1989.* Dallas: Degolyer and MacNaughton.

DeGrasse, R. W. 1983. *Military Expansion Economic Decline, The Impact of Military Spending on United States Economic Performance.* Armonk, N.Y.: M. E. Sharpe.

Dennis, J. R. 1978. "Roll-call Votes and National Security: Focusing on the Freshman." *Orbis* 22:713–735.

Dennis, Jack, ed. 1984. *The Nuclear Almanac: Confronting the Atom in War and Peace.* Reading, Mass.: Addison-Wesley.

Domhoff, G. William. 1991. "American State-Autonomy via the Military? Another Counterattack on a Theoretical Delusion." *Critical Sociology* 18:9–56.

Domhoff, G. William. 1987. "The Wagner Act and Theories of the State: A New Analysis Based on Class-Segment Theory." *Political Power and Social Theory* 6:159–185.

Domhoff, G. William. 1990. *The Power Elite and the State: How Policy is Made in America.* New York: Aldine De Gruyter.

Domhoff, G. William. 1983. *Who Rules America Now? A View for the 80s.* Prentice-Hall, Inc.,

Domhoff, G. William. 1974. *The Bohemian Grove and Other Retreats: A Study of Ruling-Class Cohesiveness.* New York: Harper and Row.

Domhoff, G. William. 1970. *The Higher Circles: The Governing Class in America.* New York: Vintage Books.

Domke, William K., Richard C. Eichenberg, and Catherine M. Kelleher. 1983. "The Illusion of Choice: Defense and Welfare in Advanced Industrial Democracies, 1948–1978." *American Political Science Review* 77:19–35.

Dumenil, G., M. Glick, and J. Rangel. 1987. "The Rate of Profit in the United States." *Cambridge Journal of Economics* 11:331–359.

Durie, S., and R. Edwards. 1982. *Fueling the Nuclear Arms Race, the Links Between Nuclear Power and Nuclear Weapons.* London: Pluto Press.

Edsall, Thomas Byrne. 1984. *The New Politics of Inequality.* New York: W. W. Norton & Co.

Epstein, Edwin M. 1980. "Firm Size and Structure, Market Power and Business Political Influence: Review of the Literature" in John Siegfried (ed.), *The Economics of Firm Size, Market Structure, and Social Responsibility.* Washington, D.C.: Government Printing Office, 240–281.

Esping-Anderson, C., R. Friedland, and E. O. Wright. 1979. "Class Structure and the Capitalist State," in R. Quinney (ed.), *Capitalist Society,* Homewood, Ill.: Dorsey, 141–162.

Etzioni, Amitai. 1984. *Capital Corruption.* San Diego: Harcourt Brace Jovanovich.

Fallows, James. 1981, *National Defense.* New York: Random House.

Ferguson, Thomas, and Joel Rogers, eds. 1981. *The Hidden Election: Politics and Economics in the 1980 Presidential Campaign.* New York: Pantheon Books.

Ferguson, Thomas, and Joel Rogers. 1986. *Right Turn: The Decline of the Democrats and the Future of American Politics.* New York: Hill and Wang.

Ferrell, Robert F. 1972. "The Merchants of Death, Then and Now." *Journal of International Affairs* 26:29–39.

Forsberg, Randall. 1986. "Behind the Facade: Nuclear War and Third World Intervention." Joseph Gerson (ed.), *The Deadly Connection: Nuclear War and U.S. Intervention.* Philadelphia: New Society Publishers.

Forum Institute. 1985. *Search for Security.* Washington, D.C.: Forum Institute.

Fox, J. Ronald. 1974. *Arming America: How the United States Buys Weapons.* Cambridge, Mass.: Harvard University Press, 101.

Frankel, Boris. 1979. "On the State of the State: Marxist Theories of the State after Leninism." *Theory and Society* 7:199–242.

Freedman, Lawrence, ed. 1986. *U.S. Intelligence and the Soviet Strategic Threat.* Princeton: Princeton University Press.

Fried, Edward R., and Nanette M. Blandin. 1988. *Oil and America's Security.* Washington, D.C.: Brookings Institute.

Friedman, Col. Richard S., Bill Gunston, David Hobbs, Lt. Col. David Miller, Doug Richardson, and Max Walmer. 1985. *Advanced Technology Warfare.* New York: Harmony Books.

Gabriel, Richard A., and Paul L. Savage. 1978. *Crisis in Command: Mismanagement in the Army.* New York: Hill and Wang.

Gais, Thomas L. 1983. "On the Scope and Bias of Interest Group Involvement in Election." APSA Paper, September, 12–14.

Gamson, William A. 1975. *The Strategy of Social Protest.* Homewood, Ill.: Dorsey.

Gansler, Jacques S. 1989. *Affording Defense.* Cambridge, Mass.: The MIT Press.

Gansler, Jacques S. 1980. *The Defense Industry* Cambridge, Mass.: The MIT Press.

Gervasi, T. 1981. *Arsenal of Democracy III.* New York: Grove Press.

Gilbert, Jess and Carolyn Howe. 1991. "Beyond 'State vs. Society': Theories of the State and New Deal Agricultural Policies." *American Sociological Review* 56:204–220.

Godfrey, L. G. 1978. "Testing Against Autoregressive and Moving Average Error Models When the Regressors Include Lagged Dependent Variables." *Econometrica* 46:1293–1302.

Gold, D. 1977. "The Rise and Fall of the Keynesian Coalition." *Kapitalstate* 6:129–161.

Gold, D., C.Y.H. Lo, and E. O. Wright. 1975. "Recent Developments in Marxist Theories of the State." *Monthly Review* 27(Oct.–Nov.):29–43.

Graham, Daniel O. 1977. "The Decline of Strategic Thought." *Air Force* 60:24–29.

Gray, R. C. 1979. "Learning From History: Case Studies of the Weapons Acquisition Process." *World Politics* 31:457–470.

Gray, Colin S. 1981. "Nuclear Strategy: the Case for a Theory of Victory." *International Security* 4:54–87.

Gray, Colin S. 1978. "The SALT Syndrome." *Adelphi Papers.* London: Adelphi Institute.

Gray, R. C. 1979. "Learning from History: Case Studies of the Weapons Acquisitions Process." *World Politics* 31:457–470.

Greene, William H. 1989. *Limdeptm User's Manual.* Ann Arbor: Interuniversity Consortium for Political and Social Research.

Greenwood, T. 1975. *Making the MIRV: A Study of Defense Policymaking.* Cambridge, Mass.: Ballinger Publishing.

Grenzke, Janet M. 1989. "PACs and the Congressional Supermarket: The Currency is Complex." *American Journal of Political Science* 33:1–24.

Grey, C. H., and G. W. Gregory. 1968. "Military Spending and Senate Voting." *Journal of Peace Research* 5:45–54.

Griffin, L. J., M. Wallace, and J. Devine. 1982a. "Monopoly Capital, Organized Labor, and Military Expenditures in the United States, 1946–1976." *American Journal of Sociology (Supplement)* 88:S113–S153.

Griffin, L. J., M. Wallace, and J. Devine. 1982b. "The Political Economy of Military Spending: Evidence from the United States." *Cambridge Journal of Economics* 6:1–14.

Halperin, M. 1972. "The Decision to Deploy the ABM: Bureaucratic Politics in the Johnson Administration." *World Politics* 25:62–93.

Hamblin, R. L., M. Hout, J. L. L. Miller, and B. L. Pitcher. 1977. "Arms Races: A Test of Two Models." *American Journal of Sociology* 42:338–354.

Harries-Jenkins, G., and C. C. Moscos, Jr. 1981. "Armed Forces and Society." *Current Sociology*, 23(3) (Wtr.).

Harvey, A. C., and I. D. McAvinchey. 1981. "On the Relative Efficiency of Various Estimators of Regression Models with Moving Average Disturbances," in E. G. Charatsis (ed.), *Proceedings of the Econometric Society European Meetings*, Athens, 1979. North Holland.

Heise, J. P. 1979. *Minimum Disclosure: How the Pentagon Manipulates the News*. New York: W. W. Norton.

Himmelstein, J. L. and D. Clawson. 1984. "The Rise of Corporate Conservatism," unpublished manuscript, University of Massachusetts, Amherst.

Himmelstein, Jerome L. 1990. *To the Right: the Transformation of American Conservatism*. Berkeley: University of California Press.

Holland, Lauren H. 1985. "The Use of NEPA in Defense Policy Politics: Public and State Involvement in the MX Missile Project." *The Social Science Journal* 21(3):53–71.

Holland, Lauren H., and Robert A. Hoover. 1985. *The MX Decision: A New Direction in US. Weapons Procurement Policy?* Boulder, Colo.: Westview Press.

Hollist, W. L. 1977, "Alternative Explanations of Competitive Arms Processes: Tests on Four Pairs of Nations." *American Journal of Political Science* 21:313–340.

Hooks, Gregory. 1990a. "The Rise of the Pentagon and U.S. State Building: The Defense Program as Industrial Policy." *American Journal of Sociology* 96:358–404.

Hooks, Gregory. 1990b. "The Variable Autonomy of the State: A Comment on 'Steel and the State'." *American Sociological Review* 56:557–560.

Hooks, Gregory. 1991. *Forging the Military-Industrial Complex: World War II's Battle of the Potomac*. Chicago: University of Illinois Press.

Horowitz, David. 1969. *Corporations and the Cold War*. New York: Monthly Review Press.

Hudson, George E., and Joseph Kruzel, eds. 1985. *American Defense Annual*. Lexington, Mass.: Lexington Books.

Hunter, Allen. 1981. "In the Wings: New Right Ideology and Organization." *Radical America* 15:113–138.

Huntington, Samuel. P. 1961. "Inter-service Competition and the Political Role of the Armed Services." *American Political Science Review* 55:50–52.

Isaac, Larry W., and Larry J. Griffin. 1989. "Ahistoricsim in Time-Series Analyses of Historical Process: Critique, Redirection, and Illustrations from U.S. Labor History." *American Sociological Review* 54:873–890.

International Institute for Strategic Studies. 1991. *The Military Balance 1991–1992.* London: Brassey for International Institute for Strategic Studies.

Jacobs, David. 1988. "Corporate Economic Power and the State: A Longitudinal Assessment of Two Explanations." *American Journal of Sociology* 93(January):852–881.

Jacoby, H. 1973. *The Bureaucratization of the World.* Berkeley: University of California.

Jenkins, J. Craig, and Barbar G. Brents. 1989. "Social Protest, Hegemonic comptetiton, and Social Reform: A Political Struggle Interpretation of the Origins of the American Welfare State." *American Sociological Review* 54:891–909.

Johnston, J. 1984. *Econometric Methods, 3rd Edition.* New York: McGraw-Hill.

Jones, Thomas K., and W. Scott Thompson. 1978. "Central War and Civil Defense." *Orbis* 22:682–712.

Joseph, P. and S. Rosenblum, eds. 1984. *Search for Sanity, the Politics of Nuclear Weapons.* Boston: South End Press.

Judge, George G., William E. Griffiths, R. Carter Hill, and Tsoung-Chao Lee. 1980. *The Theory and Practice of Econometrics.* New York: John Wiley and Sons.

Kachigan, Sam. 1982. *Multivariate Statistical Analysis.* New York: Radius Press.

Kaldor, Mary. 1981. *The Baroque Arsenal.* New York: Hill and Wang.

Kanter, Arnold. 1975. *Defense Politics, A Budgetary Perspective.* Chicago: University of Chicago Press.

Kaufman, R. F. 1972. *The War Profiteers.* New York: Doubleday and Co.

Kennedy, G. 1983. *Defense Economics.* New York: St. Martins Press.

Kennedy, G. 1975. *The Economics of Defense.* New York: St. Martins Press.

Kessler, Ronald C., and David F. Greenberg. 1981. *Linear Panel Analysis: Models of Quantitative Change.* New York: Academic Press.

Klandermans, Bert, ed. 1991. *Peace Movements in International Perspective.* 3:263–282

Koistinen, P.A.C. 1980. *The Military Industrial Complex, A Historical Perspective.* New York: Praeger Books.

Kolko, Gabriel. 1963. *Main Currents in Modern American History.* New York: Harper and Row.

Korb, L. F. 1981. "Defense Budget Processes and Defense Policy." *Armed Forces and Society* 7:317–321.

Kotz, Nick. 1988. *Wild Blue Yonder: Money, Politics, and the B-1 Bomber.* New York: Pantheon Books.

Kurth, James R. 1973. "Aerospace Production Lines and American Defense Spending." In Steven Rosen (ed.) *Testing the Theory of the Military-Industrial Complex.* Lexington, Mass.: Lexington Books.

Kurth, James R. 1978. "Hand in Glove with the Pentagon: How Aerospace Contractors Keep the Lines Rolling." *MBA* (June/July):47.

Lambelet, J. C. 1975. "Do Arms Races Lead to War." *Journal of Peace Research* 12(2):123–128.

Lang, K. 1972. *Military Institutions and the Sociology of War.* London: Sage Publications.

Lapp, R. E. 1970. *Arms Beyond Doubt: The Tyranny of Weapons Technology.* New York: Cowles Book Co.

Leffler, Melvyn P. 1984. "The American Conception of National Security and the Beginnings of the Cold War, 1945–1948." *American Historical Review* 89(1):346–381.

Leidy, Michael P. and Robert W. Staiger. 1985. "Economic Issues and Methodology in Arms Race Analysis" *American Journal of Sociology* 76:562–584.

Lens, S. 1970. *The Military-Industrial Complex.* London: Stanmore Press.

Lewy, Guenter. 1978. *America in Vietnam.* New York: Oxford University Press.

Lieberson, S. 1971. "An Empirical Study of Military-Industrial Complex Linkages." *American Journal of Sociology* 76:562–585.

Lischka, Johannes R. 1977. "Armor Plate: Nickel and Steel, Monopoly and Profit." In Benjamin Franklin Cooling (ed.), *War, Business and American Society.* Port Washington, N.Y.: Kennikat Press.

Lucas, W. A. and R. H. Dawson. 1974. *The Organizational Politics of Defense.* Occasional Papers #2, Pittsburgh: International Studies Association.

Lundberg, Ferdinand. 1988. *The Rich and the Super Rich: A Study of Money and Power and Who Really Owns America.* Secaucus, N.J.: Lyle Stuart Inc.

Luttwak, Edward. 1978. "Why Arms Control Has Failed." *Commentary* (January):19–28.

Lydenberg, Steven D. 1980. *Bankrolling Ballots 1979.* New York: Council on Economic Priorities.

Lydenberg, Steven D. 1981. *Bankrolling Ballots, Update 1980.* New York: Council on Economic Priorities.

MacDougall, John. 1991. "The Freeze Movement, Congress, and the M-X Missile: Processes of Citizen Influence." In Bert Klandermans (ed.), *Peace Movements in International Perspective* 3:263–282

MacDougall, John. 1990. "Congress and the Campaign to Stop the MX Missile" in Sam Marullo and John Lofland (eds.), *Peace Action in the Eighties: Social Science Perspectives.* New Brunswick, N.J.: Rutgers University Press.

Majeski, S. J. 1983. "Mathematical Models of the United States Military Expenditure Decision-Making Process." *American Journal of Political Science* 27:485–514.

Mann, M. 1984. "Capitalism and Militarism," in Martin Shaw (ed.). *War, State, and Society.* London: Macmillan Press.

Mayer, Kenneth R. 1991. *The Political Economy of Defense Contracting.* New Haven, Conn.: Yale University Press.

Marullo, Sam and John Lofland, eds. 1990. *Peace Action in the Eighties: Social Science Perspectives.* New Brunswick, N.J.: Rutgers University Press.

Mayhew, David R. 1974. *Congress: The Election Connection.* New Haven, Conn.: Yale University Press.

McConnell, Grant. 1966. *Private Power and American Democracy.* New York: Knopf.

McCleary, Richard, and Richard A. Hays, Jr. 1980. *Applied Time Series Analysis for the Social Sciences.* Beverly Hills, Calif.: Sage Publications.

McCrea, Frances B., and Gerald E. Markle. 1989. *Minutes to Midnight: Nuclear Weapons Protest in America.* London: Sage.

McLauchlan, Gregory. 1988. "Nuclear Weapons and the Formation of the National Security State." Ph.D. dissertation. University of California, Berkeley, Department of Sociology.

McQuaid, Kim. 1976. "The Business Advisory Council of the Department of Commerce, 1933–1961: A Study in Corporate Governmental Relations." in Paul Uselding (ed.), *Research in Economic History* 1:141–197.

Melman, S. 1970. *Pentagon Capitalism, the Political Economy of War.* New York: McGraw-Hill Book Co.

Mikdashi, Zuhayr. 1986. *Transnational Oil: Issues, Policies, and Perspectives.* New York: St. Martin's Press.

Miles, Robert H. 1987. *Managing the Corporate Social Environment: A Grounded Theory.* Englewood Cliffs, N.J.: Prentice-Hall.

Miliband, Ralph. 1977. *Marxism and Politics.* New York: Oxford University Press.

Miliband, Ralph. 1969. *The State in Capitalist Society: An Analysis of Power.* New York: Basic Books.

Mills, C. W. 1956. *The Power Elite.* New York: Oxford University Press.

Mintz, Alex and Beth Hicks. 1984. "Military Keynesianism in the U.S. 1949–1976: Disaggregating Expenditures and Their Determination," *American Journal of Sociology* 90:411–417.

Mintz, Beth, and Michael Schwartz. 1985. *The Power Structure of American Business.* Chicago: University of Chicago Press.

Mizruchi, Mark S. and Thomas Koenig. 1986. "Economic Sources of Corporate Political Consensus: An Examination of Interindustry Relations." *American Sociological Review* 51(August):482–491.

Moll, K. D., and G. M. Luebbert. 1980. "Arms Race and Military Expenditure Models: A Review." *Journal of Conflict Resolution* 24:153–185.

Morehead, Joe. 1975. "Federal Advisory Committees and Access to Public Information: A Status Report." *Government Publications Review* 2:1–7.

Morris, Aldon. 1984. *The Origins of the Civil Rights Movement.* Chicago: Free Press.

Moskos, Charles C., Jr. 1974. "The Concept of the Military-Industrial Complex: Radical Critique or Liberal Bogey." *Social Problems* 21:498–512.

Muscative, Alison. 1986. "Georgetown University and Its Media Stars: Are They Promoting the School's Reputation or the Conservative Cause?" *The Washington Post National Weekly Edition,* 10–11.

Muskie, Edmund. 1976. *VIII National Journal.* (September 18) #38, 1300

Nathanson, Charles E. 1969. "The Militarization of the American Economy." In David Horwitz (ed.), *Corporations and the Cold War.* New York: Monthly Review Press.

Neter, John, and William Wasserman. 1974. *Applied Linear Statistical Models.* Georgetown, Ontario: Irwin-Dorsey Ltd.

Newey, Whitney K. and Kenneth D. West. 1987. "A Simple, Positive, Semi-definite, Heteroskedasticity and Autocorrelation Consistent Covariance Matrix." *Econometrica* 55:703–703.

Nincic, Miroslav. 1982. *The Arms Race: The Political Economy of Military Growth.* New York: Praeger.

Nincic, M, and Cusock, T. 1979. "The Political Economy of United States Military Spending." *Journal of Peace Research* 10:101–15.

Nitze, Paul. 1976–77. "Deterring Our Deterrent." *Foreign Policy* 25(Winter):194–210.

O'Connor, James. 1973. *The Fiscal Crisis of the State.* New York: St. Martins Press.

Offe, C. and Volker Ronge. 1982. "Theses on the Theory of the State." In A. Giddens and D. Held (eds.), *Classes, Power, and Conflict.* Berkeley: University of California Press, 240–256.

Office of Technology Assessment. 1986. *Strategic Defenses: Ballistic Missile Defense*

Technologies, Anti-Satellite Weapons, Countermeasures, and Arms Control. Washington, D.C.: U.S. Government Printing Office.

Ostrom, C. W. 1977. "Evaluating Alternative Foreign Policy Models: An Empirical Test Between an Arms Race Model and An Organizational Politics Model." *Journal of Conflict Resolution* 21:235–265.

Owens, J. E. 1986. "The Impact of Campaign Contribution on Legislative Outcomes: Evidence from a House Committee." *Political Studies* 34(June):285–295.

Pipes, Richard. 1977. "Why the Soviet Union Thinks it Could Fight and Win a Nuclear War." *Commentary* 64(1):21–34.

Pittman, Russell. 1977. "Market Structure and Campaign Contributions." *Public Choice* 31:37–52.

Piven, Francis F. and Richard Cloward. 1979. *Poor People's Movements.* New York: Pantheon.

Poulantzas, Nicos. 1980. *State, Power, Socialism.* London: New Left.

Poulantzas, Nicos. 1978. *Classes in Contemporary Capitalism.* London: Verso.

Poulantzas, Nicos. 1973. *Political Power and Social Class.* London: New Left Books.

Poulantzas, Nicos. 1972. "The Problem of the Capitalist State." In Robin Blackburn (ed.), *Ideology in the Social Sciences.* New York: Vintage. 238–253.

Prados, John. 1982. *The Soviet Estimate: US Intelligence Analysis and Russian Military Strength.* New York: Dial Press.

Prados, John. 1986. *Presidents' Secret Wars: CIA and Pentagon Covert Operations Since World War II.* New York: William Morrow and Co.

Prechel, Harland. 1990. "Conflict and Historical Variation in Steel Capital-State Relations: The Emergence of State Structures and a More Prominent, Less Autonomous State." *American Sociological Review* 56:560–565.

President's Air Policy Commission. 1948. *Survival in the Air Age: A Report by the President's Air Policy Commission.* Washington, D.C.: Government Printing Office.

Priest, T. B., Richard T. Sylves, and David F. Scudder. 1984. "Corporate Advice: Large Corporations and Federal Advisory Committees." *Social Science Quarterly* 65:100–111.

Pursell, Carroll W., Jr. 1972. *The Military Industrial Complex.* New York: Harper and Row.

Quadagno, J. S. 1984. "Welfare Capitalism and the Social Security Act of 1935." *American Sociological Review* 49(Oct.):632–647.

Reed, L. S. 1975. *Military Maneuvers: An Analysis of the Interchange of Personnel Between Defense Contractor and the Department of Defense.* Washington, D.C.: Council on Economic Priorities.

Roose, Diana. 1975. *Politics, Position, and Power, 2nd Edition.* New York: Oxford University Press.

Rosen, S. 1973. "Introduction." *Testing Theories of the Military-Industrial Complex.* Lexington, Mass.: D. C. Heath and Co.

Rosenthal, Robert and Ralph L. Rosnow. 1987. *Contrast Analysis: Focused Comparisons in the Analysis of Variance.* New York: Cambridge University Press.

Roy, Wiliam G. 1981. "The Vesting of Interests and the Determinants of Political Power: Size Network Structure, and Mobilizations of American Industries 1886–1905." *American Journal of Sociology* 86:1287–1310.

Roy, Wiliam G. 1977. "Inter-Industry Vesting in a National Polity over Time: The United States 1886–1905." Ph.D. dissertation, University of Michigan.

Sale, Kirkpatrick. 1976. *Power Shift: The Rise of the Southern Rim and its Challenge to the Eastern Establishment.* New York:: Vintage Books.

Sanders, Jerry W. 1983. *Peddlers of Crisis: The Committee on the Present Danger and the Politics of Containment.* Boston: South End Press.

Scheer, Robert. 1982. *With Enough Shovels: Reagan, Bush, and Nuclear War.* New York: Random House.

Shaw, M., ed. 1984. "Introduction." *War, State, and Society.* London: Macmillan Press.

Shoup, Laurence. 1980. *The Carter Presidency and Beyond, Power and Politics in the 1980s.* Palo Alto, Calif.: Ramparts Press.

Silberman, Jonathan, and Gilbert Yochum. 1978. "The Roles of Money in Determining Election Outcomes." *Social Science Quarterly* 58:671–682.

Sivard, Ruth Leger. 1982. *World Military and Social Expenditures: 1982.* Leesburg, Va.: World Priorities.

Skocpol, Theda. 1980. "Political Response to Capitalist Crisis: Neo-Marxist Theories of the State and the New Deal." *Politics and Society* 10(2):155–201.

Skocpol, Theda, and Ann Orloff. 1984. "Why Not Equal Protection? Explaining the Politics of Public Social Welfare in Britain and the United States in the 1880s-1920s." *American Sociological Review* 49(Dec.):726–750.

Skocpol, Theda, and Edwin Amenta. 1985. "Did Capitalists Shape Social Security (Comment on Quadagno, Oct. 1984)?" *American Sociological Review* 50:572–575.

Skocpol and Kenneth Finegold. 1990. "Explaining New Deal Labor Policy." *American Political Science Review.* 84(4):1297–1304.

Smith, Carlton. 1988. "Boeing's Political Money: Who Gets it, and What Does it Buy." *The Seattle Post-Intelligencer/The Seattle Times.* September 4:Section B, 1–5.

SPSS Inc. 1988. *SPSS-X User's Guide.* 3d ed. Chicago: SPSS Inc.

Standard and Poor's Manual of Industrials. 1979. New York: H. V. Poor.

Steck, Henry J. 1975. "Private Influence on Environmental Policy: The Case of the National Industrial Pollution Control Council." *Environmental Law* 7(Winter):333–343.

Stinchombe, A. 1978. *Theoretical Methods in Social History.* London: Macmillan.

Stouffer, Samuel, Edward A. Suchman, Leland DeVinney, Shirley A. Star, and Robin M. Williams, Jr. 1949a. *The American Soldier: Adjustment During Army Life.* Volume I. Princeton: Princeton University Press.

Stouffer, Samuel A., Arthur A. Lumsdaine, Marion H. Lumsdaine, Robin M. Williams, Jr., M. Brewster Smith, Irvin L. Janis, Shirley A. Star, and Leonard S. Cottrell, Jr., 1949b. *The American Soldier: Combat and Its Aftermath.* Volume II. Princeton: Princeton University Press.

Strauss, Anselm L. 1990. *Basics of Qualitative Research: Grounded Theory Procedures and Techniques.* Newbury Park, Calif.: Sage Publications.

Stubbing, Richard A., and Richard A. Mendel. 1986. *The Defense Game: An Insider Explores the Astonishing Realities of America's Defense Establishment.* New York: Harper and Row.

Tamman, R. L. 1973. *MIRV and the Arms Race, An Interpretation of Defense Strategy.* New York: Praeger Publishers.

Tarrow, Sydney. 1983. "Struggling to Reform: Social Movements and Policy Change

During Cycles of Protest." *Western Societies Program Occasional Paper #15.* Ithaca, N.Y.: Center for International Studies.

The New York Times. 1988. April 15, 7.

The New York Times. 1989. July 11, 11

Thee, M. 1978. "The Dynamics of the Arms Race, Military Research and Development and Disarmament." *International Social Science Journal* 30(4):904–925.

Thompson, Mark. 1986. "Lockheed Asks Its Employes to Lobby—But Under Cover." *Detroit Free Press,* June 27, 15C.

Tilly, Charles, ed. 1975. *The Formation of National States in Western Europe.* Princeton: Princeton University Press.

Tsipsis, Kosta. 1983. *Arsenal: Understanding Weapons in the Nuclear Age.* New York: Simon and Schuster.

Tsipsis, Kosta. 1982. *Arsenal: Understanding Weapons in the Nuclear Age.* New York: Simon and Schuster.

Tufte, E. 1978. *Political Control over the Economy.* Princeton: Princeton University Press.

Tyroler, Charles, II., ed. 1984. *Alerting America: The Papers of the Committee on The Present Danger.* Washington: Pergamon-Brassey's.

U.S. Arms Control and Disarmament Agency. 1983. *World Military Expenditures and Arms Transfers.* Washington, D.C.: US. Government Printing Office.

U.S. Arms Control and Disarmament Agency. 1988. *World Military Expenditures and Arms Transfers.* Washington, D.C.: U.S. Government Printing Office.

U.S. Department of Commerce. Various years. *The Statistical Abstract of the United States.* Washington, D.C.: U.S. Government Printing Office.

U.S. Department of Commerce. 1977. Bureau of Economic Analysis. *Business Statistics, Biennial Supplement to the Survey of Current Business.* Washington, D.C.: U.S. Government Printing Office.

U.S. Department of Commerce. 1984. Bureau of Economic Analysis. *Business Statistics, Biennial Supplement to the Survey of Current Business.* Washington, D.C.: U.S. Government Printing Office.

U.S. Department of Commerce. 1987. Bureau of Economic Analysis. *Business Statistics, Biennial Supplement to the Survey of Current Business.* Washington, D.C.: U.S. Government Printing Office.

U.S. Office of the Secretary of Defense. 1992. *The Defense Planning Guidance for the Fiscal Years 1994–1999.* Reprinted in *The New York Times.* Vol. CXLI, No. 48,899 (March 8, 1992). Washington, D.C.: Directorate of Information, Operations, and Research.

U.S. Office of the Secretary of Defense. Annual. *100 Companies: Companies Receiving the Largest Dollar volume of Military Prime Contract Awards: Fiscal Year 1979,* for 1975 to 1986. Washington, D.C.: Directorate of Information, Operations, and Research.

U.S. Office of the Secretary of Defense. Annual. *100 Companies and Their Subsidiaries Listed According to Net Value of Military Prime Contract Awards: Fiscal Year 1958,* for 1951 to 1974. Washington, D.C.: Directorate of Information, Operations, and Research.

U.S. Senate, Hearings before the Subcommittee on Anti-trust and Monopoly of the Committee on the Judiciary. *Competition in Defense Procurement.* 90th Congress, 2nd Session (1968), 21.

Useem, Michael. 1984. *The Inner Circle: Large Corporations and the Rise of Business Political Activity in the United States and the United Kingdom.* New York: Oxford University Press.

Useem, Michael. 1983. "Business and Politics in the United States and the United Kingdom." *Theory and Society* 12:281–300.

Useem, Michael. 1979. "The Social Organization of the American Business Elite and Participation of Corporation Directors in the Governance of American Institutions." *American Sociological Review* 44(August):553–572.

Vogel, David. 1989. *Fluctuating Fortunes: The Political Power of Business in America.* New York: Basic Books.

Walsh, Edward. 1986. "What? Who, Us? Vote Ourselves a Pay Raise?" *The Washington Post Weekly Edition.* May 5, 14.

Weir, Margaret, Ann Shola Orloff, and Theda Skocpol, eds. 1988. *The Politics of Social Policy in the United States.* Princeton: Princeton University Press.

Weisberg, Sanford. 1980. *Applied Linear Regression.* New York: Wiley.

Welch, William. 1974. "The Economics of Campaign Funds." *Public Choice* 20:83–97.

Welch, William. 1976. "The Effectiveness of Campaign Funds in State Legislative Races." *American Politics Quarterly* 4:340–343.

White, Kenneth J. Shirley A. Haun, Nancy G. Horsman, and S. Donna Wong. 1988. *SHAZAM: Econometrics Computer Program, User's Reference Manual, Version 6.1.* New York: McGraw-Hill Book Co.

Whitt, J. Allen. 1980. "Can Capitalists Organize Themselves?" In G. W. Domhoff (ed.), *Power Structure Research.* Beverly Hills, Calif.: Sage Publications.

Whitt, J. Allen. 1979. "Toward a Class Dialectical Model of Power: An Empirical Assessment of Three Competing Models of Political Power." *American Sociological Review* 44:81–100.

Whitt, J. Allen. 1982. *Urban Elites and Mass Transportation.* Princeton: Princeton University Press.

Who's Who in America. 1950–51. Willamette, Ill.: Macmillan Directory Division.

Who's Who in America. 1983. Willamette, Ill.: Macmillan Directory Division.

Who's Who in America. 1987. Willamette, Ill.: Macmillan Directory Division.

Wildavsky, A. 1979. *The Politics of the Budgetary Process,* 3rd ed. Boston: Little Brown.

Winkler and William L. Hays. 1975. *Statistics: Probability, Inference, and Decisionmaking.* New York: Holt, Rienhart, and Winston.

Yarmolinsky, A. 1971. *The Military Establishment.* New York: Harper Colophon Books.

Yarmolinsky, A. and G. Foster. 1983. *Paradoxes of power: The Military in the Eighties.* Bloomington: Indiana University Press.

Yergin, Daniel. 1978. *Shattered Peace: The Origins of the Cold War and the National Security State.* Boston: Houghton Mifflin Co.

Zald, M, and I. Berg. 1978. "Business and Society." *Annual Review of Sociology* 4:115–143.

INDEX

Adams, Walter, 25
advisory councils and committees, 29
AFL-CIO, 55
Agent Orange, 174n12
American Enterprise Institute for Public Policy, 45
American Republic Aviation, 32
American Security Council, 33
A. Philip Randolph Institute, 46
arms race models, 7, 100
AT&T, 30
Atlantic Council, 46
autocorrelation (serial correlation), 99, 103, 104, 105, 108, 131, 138

B-1 bomber, 36, 37, 39
bail-outs, of defense firms, 26, 122
Baran, Paul, 3, 84, 125, 142
Barnet, Richard, 8
Bechtel Corporation, 33, 35
Bellow, Saul, 46
Block, Fred, 130
Boeing, 25, 26, 33
Boeing Political Action Committee (BPAC), 39
Bohemian Grove, 59
Bonferoni corrections, 104, 105
Box-Pierce Q statistic, 104, 134
Brennan, Donald G., 64
Brookings Institute, 46
budgetary inertia (bureaucratic inertia), 78, 88, 121; and autocorrelation, 138

budgetary politics, 76, 78, 89, 115
bureaucratic politics and competition, 77, 78, 79, 115
Business Council, 46
business influence on public policy, 21; institutionalized in U.S. foreign policy apparatus, 136; political behavior as product marketing, 28
Business Roundtable, 46

Cabot, John M., 59, 62, 175n3
campaign donations, 37
capitalist crisis, 86, 133, 143
capitalists, "southern rim" vs. "eastern establishment," 11
Carter, Jimmy, 17, 18, 45, 63, 66, 80, 125, 130
Casey, William, 68
Chappell, William, 37
Chrysler Corporation, 122, 175n5
class conflict and class politics, 144
clubs, upper-class social, 56, 59
Colvin, C. H., 32
Committee on Economic Development, 46
Committee on the Present Danger (CPD), 13, 33, 127, 129, 132, 140, 142; accomplishments, 66, 68, 69; activity, 71–74, 109, 111, 115, 121, 125, 127, 131, 134, 141, 143; decline, 70, 71; goals, 65; organizations affiliated with, 63, 64; resources, 62